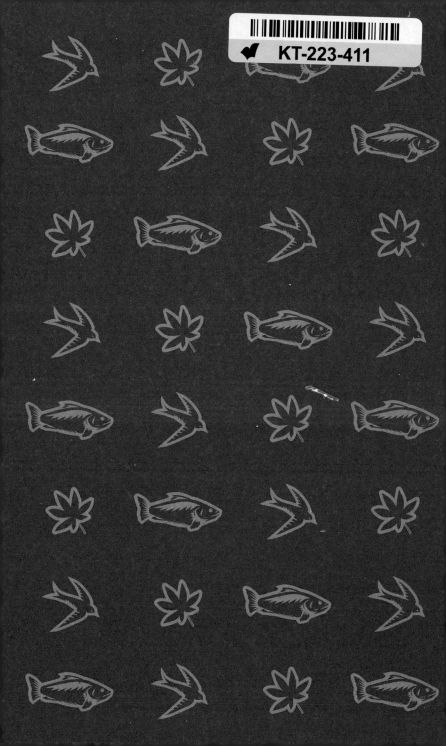

WRITTEN BY CHRIS STEVENS
ILLUSTRATED BY A.J. GARCES
(WITH ADDITIONAL ILLUSTRATIONS BY DAVID WOODROFFE)

EDITED BY RACHEL CARTER
DESIGNED BY ZOE QUAYLE

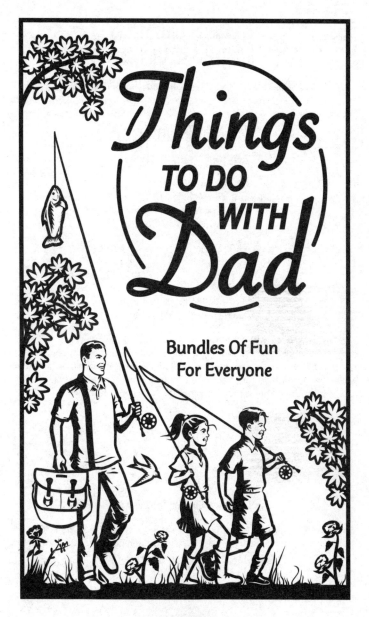

Things TO DO WITH Dad

Bundles Of Fun For Everyone

Michael O'Mara Books Limited

First published in Great Britain in 2008 by Michael O'Mara Books Limited,
9 Lion Yard, Tremadoc Road, London SW4 7NQ
www.mombooks.com

A CIP catalogue record for this book is available from
the British Library.

ISBN: 978-1-906082-20-8

2 4 6 8 10 9 7 5 3 1

Printed and bound in England by Clays Ltd, St Ives plc

Papers used by Michael O'Mara Books are natural, recyclable products made from wood grown in sustainable forests. The manufacturing processes conform to the environmental regulations of the country of origin.

Contents

Introduction

Free time is ten times more fun when it is shared. Whatever games and activities you dream up, they take on a whole new meaning when Dad and the kids get involved. So whether it's the weekend, the holidays or that precious free hour at the end of a busy day, here are dozens of ideas for activities that will have everyone grinning from ear to ear.

If you've got energy to burn, this book contains sports and games ideas to exercise both mind and muscles. If it's new toys you want, there are all sorts of ingenious and inexpensive playthings to make within these pages. If you need ideas for indoor fun, there's lots to do when it's raining outside. And if you want to sneak a little education into playtime, you'll even find a few facts hidden among the fun.

There are hand symbols throughout to ensure fingers get muddy and sticky but not hurt.

 This symbol indicates tasks that are best carried out by Dad, such as using matches and sharp tools.

 This symbol is for tasks that kids will particularly enjoy.

So, what are you waiting for? It's 'Dad-time' ... make the most of it!

Turn Your Kitchen Into Dad's Diner

Feeling peckish? Don't queue up at a fast food restaurant when you can cook up a delicious and nutritious feast in your own kitchen. Homemade burgers taste great, and are inexpensive to make, and mind-blowing milkshakes can be whipped up in an instant.

THE MOST AMAZING BURGERS IN THE WORLD

For four large burgers you will need:

- 450 g lean minced beef or lamb
- 4 burger buns
- 1 egg
- 2 spring onions
- 1 small onion
- a generous splash of tomato sauce
- 3 cloves of garlic
- 1 tsp chopped thyme
- 1 tsp chopped parsley
- olive oil
- butter or low-fat spread
- a pinch of salt and pepper

For the filling you will need:

- chopped lettuce, radishes and raw onion
- sliced pickled gherkin
- salad dressing

GET COOKING

 Slice the spring onions and finely chop the other onion and the garlic.

Crack the egg into a large bowl and beat it with a fork.

Put the mince in a large bowl. Using a wooden spoon, mix in the egg and the onion (not the spring onions though – you'll need those later). As you stir, add the garlic, herbs, salt and pepper, and the tomato sauce. Then use clean fingers to squelch the mix together.

Slap the mixture onto a chopping board and roll it into a slab just over 1 cm thick.

Divide the slab into four pieces and shape each one into a disk with your hands. Don't squeeze them into balls, though, they have to stay flat.

Coat the bottom of a frying pan with olive oil. Heat the oil until it is really hot, before adding the raw burgers. Fry the burgers on each side for five minutes or until cooked through.

Garnish the top of each burger with the sliced spring onions.

Top tip: For added flavour, thinly slice some mature cheddar cheese. Place the cheese on top of the cooked burgers and lightly grill until the cheese starts to bubble.

THE SHOWDOWN

Put a layer of butter or low fat spread on your buns, and slip a burger in each one.

Now it's time to get creative – add chopped lettuce, radishes, raw onion, sliced pickled gherkin and salad dressing. Turn your meal into a masterpiece with these or any fillings you fancy.

GREAT SHAKES

Banana and chocolate milkshakes make the perfect burger accompaniments. So go ahead, place your order.

For each person you will need:

- half a glass of skimmed milk
- a ripe chopped banana
- 3 dessertspoons of chocolate syrup
- ½ tsp of vanilla extract
- straws

Pour the milk into a blender and add the chocolate syrup. Make sure the cover is properly secured, then start the blender on a low speed.

When the two are thoroughly mixed, switch the blender off and add the banana and vanilla extract.

Blend again until the the shake looks creamy and spectacular.

Pour the milkshake into a tall glass and pop a straw in it.

Top tip: Instead of adding banana to the mix, if you're feeling adventurous, try a dollop of peanut butter. Or, leave out the chocolate syrup and add a good handful of strawberries with the banana.

For the final touch, decorate paper napkins with 'DD' in big capital letters. That's the logo for 'Dad's Diner'. Next stop, 'DD' restaurants worldwide ...

Create A Crazy Golf Course

Guess what? Your home is a crazy golf green just waiting to happen and you're guaranteed free membership to this course.

All the materials you'll need to build the course are within arms' reach. The aim of the game is to knock the ball into a saucepan or frying pan – but first you have to hit tricky targets and find your way around all kinds of obstacles.

Half the fun of this game is designing the course and steering clear of its traps.

You will need:

- a long umbrella, a walking stick or a hockey stick to use as your golf club • saucepans and/or frying pans • lots of obstacles, such as books and tin cans • a tennis ball

SAFE-TEE TIPS

Before you 'tee off', hide anything breakable. It is a good idea to use a tennis ball instead of a real golf ball, but stay right away from rooms with expensive, fragile objects, such as televisions. When you are playing, remember to tap the ball lightly – it makes your stroke so much more accurate.

A COURSE IN DESIGN

Now you're ready to set up a series of challenging holes. Use a combination of objects such as tin cans, books, shoes and rows of toy cars, or try building these holes:

The CD Challenge: Zigzag between pairs of CD covers balanced on their sides, but don't knock any over!

The Bath Bunker: The bathroom course starts in the bath – now renamed 'the bunker'. Instead of trying to play your way out of the bath by hitting the ball straight up the side, try aiming for the end opposite the taps.

Tin Can Alley: Tin cans make great building blocks for bridges and tunnels. Before the ball lands in a hole, hit it through a series of tin can bridges in the right order. Hole too soon, and you have to go back to the start.

Roll Up, Roll Up: The ball must travel through a triangular tunnel of books, then bounce off a marked spot on the skirting board, roll down an avenue of toy cars, slip between two shoes without touching them, and roll up another book into a saucepan.

You don't need to build *all* your holes. Why not put one under a bed? If you have stairs make them a central part of your course. Tell players they must hit the ball down the stairs and into an awaiting saucepan.

Old lengths of guttering are great for hitting the ball onto chairs or around tight corners.

MARVELLOUS MARBLE GOLF

If space is tight, try playing desktop crazy golf using a marble as a ball. Hit it with a pencil through a maze of books, tins and toys, or flick it with a fingertip along a path of rulers and cardboard tubes.

WHAT'S THE SCORE?

However you play, keep count of the number of times each player hits the ball before finishing the course. Add five penalty points to this score whenever obstacles are missed out or knocked down.

Once all the players have completed the course, the player with the lowest score wins.

Tricky Twist: Once in a game, each player can insist that their opponent wears a blindfold for a crucial shot.

Turn A Tin Can Into A Lantern

For a seriously spooky
Halloween party or
a magical outdoor
barbecue, glowing
lanterns are a
must-have.

Here's how to make a
fantastic lantern from
an empty tin can.

You will need:

• a clean, empty tin can (the type which is opened with
a ring-pull is best as it is less likely to have a sharp rim)
• a marker pen • a hammer • nails • a wire coat hanger
• wire cutters • a pair of pliers • a candle

Using the marker pen, draw a pattern of dots on
the can. You could draw a skull-and-crossbones,
hearts and diamonds, or a firework starburst. Let your
imagination run riot.

Mark two big dots on opposite sides of the tin just below the top rim. These mark the position of the holes you will use to attach the wire handle.

Fill the can with water to the brim and carefully stand it upright in the freezer. You need the water in the can to turn into a solid lump of ice because this prevents the can buckling when you start punching holes in it. Be prepared to wait at least 24 hours for the water to freeze completely.

When it's ready, place the can on a firm surface, such as a workbench, and bang a nail into the side through one of the dots. Then use the pliers to carefully pull the nail out of the can leaving a hole. Try using different sized nails to make holes of varying size.

Repeat this process until you've made all the holes.

Now stand the can in a bowl of warm water until you can remove the ice.

To make the handle, cut a length of wire from the coat hanger and bend it into a U-shape. Hook the wire through the holes at the top of the can, and bend the ends over with the pliers to secure them.

Dry out your lantern and put an unlit candle inside it (the holes on the inside will be jagged so watch your fingers). Light the candle carefully.

Watch with wonder as the light shines through the holes.

Build A Snow Fort

Snowmen are so last season! Instead, build a snow fort. This will give you a huge sense of satisfaction and put Dad's DIY snow skills to the test. Best of all, you'll end up with a secure base for staging the most awesome snowball fight ever.

You will need:

- lots of snow
- a long stick
- a large square or rectangular plastic mould, such as a recycling box or storage box
- 3 pieces of wood for door supports
- 1 piece of board for window supports
- a scarf and a short stick • an old blanket

Optional:

- Some fun shaped moulds
- a piece of sturdy board
(big enough to make a platform to stand on)

BUILDING TECHNIQUES

Scout around for a prime spot to build the fort. You are looking for flat ground, in an open space, with a plentiful supply of deep snow. Mark out the base of your fort by dragging the stick through the snow to make a large square or circle.

Fill the mould with snow, stamping it down as you go. When the snow is tightly packed, carefully turn the mould over and stamp on the base of the box to release your first snow brick.

Repeat this process until you have enough bricks to mark out the base of the fort. Don't forget to leave space for the door.

Join the bricks together by pressing snow into the gaps between each one, just like the mortar in a brick wall.

If necessary, use a kitchen knife to cut the snow bricks to size.

Next, put a layer of snow on top of the first row of bricks before building the second tier. Make sure each new brick overlaps the bricks on the row below, rather than lining up with them.

When the fort is three bricks high, dig a small hole either side of the doorway. Push a wooden door support into each hole so that it stands upright. Check each support is deeply rooted in the snow, so that it will stay in place.

Leave a gap for a window, so you can spy on your snowballing enemies. Before building a layer of bricks on top of the window, lay the window board across the gap.

Once the walls are high enough, rest the last piece of door board across the space you have left for the door. This will support the layer of bricks that are laid on top.

Add more layers until the fort is high enough to act as a shield against sneaky snowballs, but low enough for you to see over.

FINISHING TOUCHES

Tie a scarf to a stick to make a flag. Carefully push your flag into the top of the fort wall. Lay an old blanket on the floor of the fort.

Find a pile of snow and make a stash of snowballs. Take some snowballs into the fort and line them up on the fort wall. Leave a few outside for the fort's attackers.

Let the snowball fight commence!

Top tips: For a really impressive fort, make a step that you can climb up on to hurl snowballs. Once a wall is about two bricks high, build several vertical supports behind it from snow bricks carefully stacked on top of each other. Rest a board on top of the wall and the new supports. Now you have the perfect vantage point for hurling your snowballs. Just make sure it's stable before you climb on top.

Ice cream containers, plant pots or buckets make great decorative snow bricks. So, when you've finished building your fort, why not add a layer of these bricks?

FORT WARNING

Check your fort regularly to make sure it is standing strong. You don't want it to fall down on you in the middle of a snowball battle.

Bad Spelling Bee

Anyone can learn to spell well, but it takes talent to get words seriously wrong by spelling them as they sound. For example you could spell 'potato' 'ghoughpteighbteau'. Here's where the sounds for this awful spelling come from:

Letter	Sound	Example
P	gh	as in hiccou**gh**
O	ough	as in th**ough**
T	pt	as in **pt**olemy
A	eigh	as in n**eigh**
T	bt	as in de**bt**
O	eau	as in bur**eau**

Or how about spelling 'usage' 'youzitch'. This packs seven errors into a five letter word. Can you beat that?

HOW TO PLAY

Dad challenges each player to come up with a word and devise the worst spelling they can for it. The players then have two minutes to come up with their final worst spelling and write it down.

Dad looks at each player's word and must be able to guess what the word is even though it is badly spelt. Players score one point for each wrong letter they managed to fit into the word.

Good words to start with are: Australia, diamond, fatigue, height, leopard, mayonnaise, mnemonic, rhinoceros, xylophone and zucchini.

Have a Keepie-Uppie Competition

If you want to look like an international football star from a television advert, you need to master the 'keepie-uppie'. Think of it as juggling a football with your feet.

Stand on one leg with your other foot raised, the toes higher than the heel. Drop the ball onto the flat top of your foot as you flick your toes up lightly. You are aiming to bounce the ball just a few centimetres. The knack is to make sure the ball doesn't fly forwards – if it does, you'll be lunging clumsily after it. Keep it bouncing up and spinning slightly back, towards your shin. You can even add the odd knee bounce now and again.

When you've mastered the keepie-uppie, have a competition to see who can do the most in one minute. Alternatively, face each other and do keepie-uppies until one person drops their ball.

EXPERT UPPIES

Try switching feet between kicks, and letting the ball ricochet off your chest. The ultimate art is to tip your head back and launch the ball up onto your forehead – balance it there for a few seconds then let it roll back down onto your foot.

Go On A Crab-Fishing Expedition

In any seaside town or village where people have been crabbing for generations, local shops sell lines and bags of bait.

However, if you need to rustle up your own equipment, it's easy. Kite string makes a good fishing line and if it comes with a plastic handle at one end you'll have less trouble with tangling while you're angling.

The best time to catch a bucketful of crabs is when the tide is coming in. The perfect place to fish for them is from a pier or a jetty at the mouth of an estuary, where a river meets the sea.

You will need:

- a crab line • a metal hook (the top of a wire coat hanger will work fine) • a metal weight
- a large container • bait (raw bacon or squid is good)
- a fishing net

TAKE THE BAIT

Tie a piece of metal, such as a nut or bolt, near the end of your line to weigh it down.

 Tie a hook to the end of the line. It's there to hold your bait, not to catch your crustaceans, so it doesn't have to be sharp.

Bait the hook with a lump of meat about 4 cm by 4 cm. If the meat is too big, the crabs will be able to tear chunks off it. If it is too small, they won't be tempted to nibble at all. The crabs will grab the bait with their pincers, so don't worry, they won't get hurt by the hook.

Always wash your hands thoroughly after handling the bait.

Half-fill the container with water and put it to one side. Then lower the baited line until it's on the estuary bed.

If you feel a gentle tug on your line, slowly pull up your line. Don't jerk it. If there is a crab on board, get someone to hold a fishing net ready to scoop the crab up when it comes out of the water. Place the crab in your container, being careful of those pesky pincers.

Repeat until you have a container full of crabs.

At the end of the expedition, carefully pour the crabs back into the water. Don't make them crabby by keeping them out of the water for too long.

Top tips: Crabs prefer meat with a strong whiff, so you'll catch more crabs with bacon that's past its sell-by date, than fresh chicken. If the bacon is streaky, pull the fat off – otherwise the fat will float, making the bait harder for the crabs to grab.

CRABBY CONTESTS

Crabbing contests are great fun with everyone getting their own line, bait and bucket.

First To Five: The first person to catch five crabs wins. The crabs must make it into the bucket. If they scuttle away or fall off the line it doesn't count.

Biggest Crab Wins: Set a time limit. The person with the biggest specimen in their bucket at the end of that time is the winner.

Play Indoor Fishing

With this game, you can go on a fishing trip come rain or shine. Just don't try eating these flappy friends for supper.

For two fishermen you will need:

• 2 magnets • 2 sticks
• 2 pieces of string at least 1 m long
• a plain, medium-sized cardboard box or a
waste-paper bin • sheets of white card • sticky tape
• scissors • a box of paperclips • felt-tip pens or paints

To make a fishy template, draw a fish 15 cm long on a piece of card. Cut it out. Then make as many fish as you want by placing the template on another sheet of card, drawing around it and cutting out your catch.

 Have a competition to see who can decorate their fish the best.

Now take the box and paint waves and seaweed around the outside. If you are using a bin, decorate some sheets of A4 paper and attach them to the bin with sticky tape.

Write a number between five and ten on every fish. Then slide a paperclip over the nose of each one. Throw your shoal into the box.

To make the fishing rods, tie lengths of string to the ends of the sticks, then tie a magnet to the end of each string.

See who can score the most points by dangling their magnet in the pond and taking it in turns to catch a fish by its paperclip.

Create A Cloud

Clouds are fascinating things. They may look light and fluffy, but they are actually made from minuscule water droplets. They can move at speeds of more than 160 kilometres per hour when the wind pushes them along.

Here's how to make a cloud in your kitchen using a clear plastic two-litre bottle, a match and some water.

First, fill the bottle with hot water until it is about a third full. Put the top on the bottle and give it a good shake for a minute. As the water evaporates, water vapour will be produced in the air inside the bottle.

Unscrew the top of the bottle and hold a lit match just inside the opening for a few seconds. Drop the lit match into the bottle and immediately replace the cap. Watch as the space above the water fills with smoke and soot particles.

Give the bottle a tight squeeze then quickly release it. Keep squeezing and releasing the bottle until you see a cloud form.

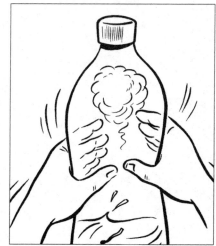

Once you have created your cloud, take the cap off the bottle and watch that little cloud escape.

Top tip: Make it easier to see the cloud by holding a sheet of black paper behind the bottle before squeezing.

THE SCIENCE BIT

In nature, a cloud is made when water vapour rises, experiences a drop in air pressure, cools and then turns into tiny water droplets. This process is helped by solid particles, such as dust or smoke, being present in the air.

In the same way, the vapour inside the bottle cools when you stop squeezing it, because this creates a drop in air pressure. The smoke inside the bottle (solid particles) helps the vapour form tiny droplets and make a cloud.

Bust An Essential Surf Move

The first time you stand up on a surfboard and ride a breaking wave will be etched on your memory forever. Anyone can learn to surf, as long as they can swim.

TAKE THE SKID TEST

Before you zip up your wetsuit and climb on your board you need to answer a very important question: are you a 'Natural' or a 'Goofy'? If you did a running slide along a polished floor would you lead with your left foot? If so, you are what surfers call 'natural-footed'. If the right foot is out front you're 'goofy-footed'. Neither is better than the other. It's all just a matter of instinct.

THE POP-UP

Here's how to master the essential surf move known as the 'pop-up'. Practise it on dry land before you even think about testing your skills in the sea.

1. Lie face down on the board. Your hands should be at your sides (shoulder-width apart), palms facing downwards and level with your chest, as if about to do a press-up. Your legs should be touching.

2. Now, in one smooth movement, push up with your hands and straighten your arms.

3. In the same moment, pull your feet and knees under your body so you are crouching on the board as shown above. Your bottom should not be touching the board. Your leading foot (the one you discovered by sliding along the floor on page 31) should be slightly in front of the other.

4. Now come up into a standing position, with one foot in front of the other, knees bent. Your feet should be just over shoulder-width apart. Your arms should be slightly bent and outstretched. Your back foot should be at a right angle to the board and the front foot at a slight diagonal. Keep your head held high and your eyes focused out front.

SURFBOARD SLANG

Now you've learnt how to stand like a surf dude, take it in turns to test each other's surf slang.

Amped – hyper, over-excited
Beached – stuffed full of food
Gnarly – a large or dangerous wave
Rails – the surfboard's curved sides
Soup – frothy white water where the wave breaks
Wipe Out – to fall from your board
Stoked – happy, excited

Make An Artificial Eye

Why not make an artificial eye to look at the world? It's amazing what you can make with an empty cardboard tube!

You will need:

- a cardboard tube (the cylinder kind with a plastic lid that keep circular potato crisps fresh – clean out any crumbs!)
- a ruler • a drawing pin • a craft knife • masking tape
- a felt-tip pen • a sheet of tracing paper • kitchen foil

With a felt-tip draw a straight line around the tube about 5 cm from the closed base.

Using a sharp craft knife, carefully cut the tube into two pieces along the line you have drawn.

With a drawing pin, poke a hole through the centre of the metal base of the tube.

Cut a circle of tracing paper that fits snugly inside the plastic lid of the tube. This will act as the screen of your 'eye'. Secure it with some tape.

Put the plastic lid (with the screen inside) back onto your tube – on the open end of the short piece of tube.

Next, put the long tube back on the other side of the lid, and tape it in place with masking tape.

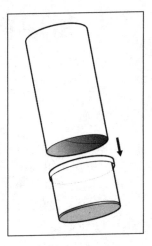

To prevent light from leaking into the tube, roll it in a double layer of kitchen foil and tape the foil tightly into place.

You should now have something that looks a little bit like a kitchen foil telescope. This is your artificial eye.

On a bright sunny day, head outside and find an object that won't move – such as a tree or building. Hold the open end of your tube to one eye. Press it firmly against your face to cut out as much light as possible.

You should be able to see a colour image that has been projected through the pin hole onto the screen. It will be an upside-down image.

Top tip: If you can't see the image clearly, try putting a blanket over your head and poking the tube out of a gap in the material. This will reduce the amount of light that can leak into the end of the tube that is in front of your eye.

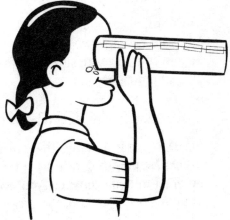

Take A Road Trip

Turn boring car journeys into a road trip and you'll never hear the words '*Are we nearly there yet?*' ever again. Here's how to make sure your four-wheeled adventure is one to remember.

DESTINATION UNKNOWN

Head for an interesting town or attraction you've never visited before, or decide on the general direction you want to head in and see where you end up. After all, the more spontaneous your trip, the greater the thrill.

Pack plenty of tasty food and drink to break the journey. Nothing tastes better than ginger beer swigged straight from the bottle and home-made apple pie eaten with your fingers.

Make a road trip soundtrack – each person brings five CDs for the open road so you can mix and match songs.

Don't be afraid to take a detour if something exciting crops up en route, such as a beautiful field or beach. Road trips are as much about the journey as the destination.

TIME FOR A CHAT

Why not take it in turns to ask each other a question that you would never ask in normal life. Try '*What was the best day of your life?*' or '*When are you happiest?*'

For a bit of light-hearted chatter, try playing a game of 'Never-Ending Story'. Take it in turns to add a sentence to a story that you make up on the spot, or give a popular fairy tale an amusing revamp. Even if you start somewhere obvious such as '*Once upon a time, there were three bears...*', the story will soon take some unexpected twists: '"*This is a stick-up. Hand over your porridge!*" *shouted Goldilocks.*'

Learn A Capoeira Move

Question: Which sport combines martial arts and dance, and improves your balance and coordination?
Answer: Capoeira – a sport invented in the 17th century in Brazil.

If you want to impress your friends with some of the coolest moves on the planet, read on.

GINGA MOVE

The Ginga is the most important move in capoeira. The word literally means 'to rock back and forward' or to swing. This basic movement is a way of keeping the body prepared for other capoeira moves.

1. Stand with your feet shoulder-width apart – this will help you maintain your balance. Raise your left arm diagonally across your body and extend your left leg behind you.

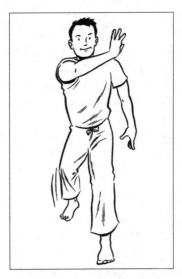

2. Then, move your left leg forward again, taking a step sideways.

3. Next, raise your right arm and extend your right leg backwards.

4. Take a step forward and to the right. Repeat this sequence.

Music is very important to capoeira, as it sets the tempo. Pop on a track. As you get into the rhythm of the move, it should start to 'swing' and your limbs will feel free and easy.

THE AU BATIDO

Now you are ready for your next move – the Au Batido, which means 'broken cartwheel'. This is a dazzling capoeira move and takes a long time to master, so be very careful when you try this variation.

Find a big, empty space, ideally outside on grass, and move any objects well out of the way.

1. With a spring in your step, turn your right foot to the side, pointing in the direction you are going to move. (If you are left-handed you will find it easier to use your left foot.)

Extend your right arm up above your head (left arm for left-handers), then fall onto your right hand as if you were doing a cartwheel.

2. Before both legs reach an upright position, twist your hips to stop the momentum of your cartwheel (this is tricky at first, but don't worry, the more you practise the easier you will find it to balance on one hand).

3. Kick your left leg towards your chest (left-handers use your right leg), so that your legs end up in a V-shape.

Use your free hand to grab hold of your leg as shown here.

4. Now let go of the leg and lower your free hand. Cartwheel back down to the ground the way you came, keeping your legs straight.

Capoeira takes a lot of practice and it is a good idea to help each other balance when learning a new move.

Once you have got the hang of it, here are some incredible shapes that professionals can achieve.

Make A Glow-In-The-Dark T-shirt

A glow-in-the-dark bat T-shirt is great for spooking your friends or neighbours on Halloween. Trick or treat!

You will need:

- a black T-shirt • glow-in-the-dark paint (available from a craft shop) • white and black fabric paint • a plate • a large potato • a small paintbrush • paper • card
- a vegetable knife • a pencil • scissors • some newspaper

Cut the potato in half lengthways using a vegetable knife.

Practise drawing the outline of a bat on a piece of paper, then draw your final design on to a piece of card. Make sure your bat is no bigger than your potato half.

Cut out the cardboard bat to make a template. Place the bat on the potato and draw around it by scoring the potato with a pencil.

With the knife, cut away the potato surrounding the bat shape, so that the bat is left raised.

Fold a newspaper in half and tuck it inside the front of your T-shirt so it is behind the spot where you will print your bat.

Pour some white paint onto a plate, and dip your 'bat-ato' into it. The surface of the bat should be covered with paint, but it should not be dripping.

Make a print on the front of the T-shirt by pressing the bat-ato firmly against the fabric. Do this once in the centre of the shirt, or several times, so the front is covered with flapping bats. Wipe your bat-ato clean.

Leave the white paint to dry. Wash the plate, then pour glow-in-the-dark paint onto the plate.

Dip your bat-ato in the paint and press it on to the white bat on the T-shirt. The glow-in-the-dark paint will really stand out when printed over the white background. When the paint has dried, paint eyes and a mouth on your bat in black fabric paint.

When the bat has dried, put on your T-shirt and get ready to look scary.

Have A Plate-Spinning Competition

Plate spinning will keep you occupied for hours. Always use plastic plates – that way you won't break the best china and injure yourself in the process.

You will need:

- plastic plates with a circular rim underneath
(they need a slightly hollow underside
that slopes in towards the centre)
- bamboo sticks or dowelling
(at least 1 m long)

GOING SOLO

Start by holding a stick at a slight angle – imagine the angle an hour hand makes when it is pointing to two o'clock.

Pick up a plate and hang it from the stick by the rim.

Make a slow circular motion with your wrist, so that the plate starts to spin. Keep the rest of your arm still. Don't move your shoulder or elbow. Make sure the plate rolls around the stick, and doesn't get stuck on one spot. It should move like a spinning top, not a swinging lasso.

Gradually rotate the plate faster and faster until it levels out and is spinning horizontally. Then stop moving the stick. It should slide to the concave centre of the plate, and for the next few seconds, hey presto, the plate will spin by itself.

Don't panic when the plate starts to slow and wobble. Just give the stick a few more flicks with your wrist.

THE TWO TIMER

Now you've mastered the basic spin, switch the stick to your free hand by sliding your grip close to the plate, lifting your leg and handing the plate under your leg for extra effect. Then place another plate on the tip of a second stick, and spin the plates two-at-a-time. Watch that the plates don't collide with each other!

IN A SPIN

Kick off a contest to see who can spin a plate the longest. Then take your act outside and see who can spin the most plates at once. Push sticks into soft earth so you won't have to struggle to hold the plates as they spin.

As you set new plates spinning, give the other sticks a flick to keep them going.

If you manage to spin more than three plates at one time, congratulations – you should be in the circus!

TOP TRICKS

Lift the spinning plate off the stick with your forefinger and hold it up high. Then flick it up in the air and catch it on the end of your finger.

Spin two plates, one in each hand. Throw both plates into the air at the same time and then catch them on the opposite stick.

If you're feeling really clever, why not make the plate spin really quickly, tip your head back, and balance the end of the stick on your chin? Practice makes perfect.

Hold A Garage Sale

A garage sale is a fun way to get rid of unwanted household clutter and turn it into cash that can help to fund a road trip, a crab-fishing expedition or perhaps the work of your favourite charity.

Before you start searching for money-spinners, read the following tips.

IT'S A DATE

A good garage sale needs a lot of planning. Your customers won't just appear by magic – you have to give them plenty of warning about your bargain bonanza.

Start by fixing a date and time for the sale as far in advance as possible – at least one month.

Pick a Saturday or Sunday if you can. Make sure your sale doesn't clash with public holidays and other events in the area, such as car boot sales and fêtes.

READ ALL ABOUT IT

 Make some colourful posters advertising the date, time and place of your sale.

Pin up your posters outside your house. Try giving some flyers to friends and neighbours. Work as a team to advertise your sale.

WHAT TO SELL

Search your house thoroughly for any unwanted items that you could sell on your stall.

Join forces to look in rooms, cupboards and under beds. Don't forget to peer into the depths of the garage and attic if you have one.

If you're not sure whether to sell something, apply this basic rule: if you've forgotten you had it, you definitely won't miss it. Just don't sell anything that isn't yours without the owner's permission!

Books, CDs, toys and kitchen utensils tend to sell easily, but don't be afraid to put every bit of junk you can find on the sales table – it might look useless to you, but it could make somebody else's day.

Clothes will sell best if you display them on a clothes rail. Cups and crockery will be bought quickly if you box them up in sets. It's easier to get rid of items such as paperbacks and CDs if you price them individually.

A long fold-down trestle table is perfect for displaying your wares.

If you're selling electrical items, such as power drills and blenders, make sure they are in safe working order first. Keep an extension lead handy to show customers that the items work properly.

Be prepared to man the stall all day in order to maximise your takings and make sure young vendors are supervised at all times.

THE PRICE IS RIGHT

Don't price too high. Be prepared to haggle with customers and always sell at a low price if the alternative is no sale at all. After all, if you didn't want to sell it, what's it doing on the table?

Tags and stickers can be off-putting, but if something is a real bargain, why not display its price?

Top tip: To get your stall noticed and have some extra fun, why not give your sale a theme. If it's Halloween, dress up in scary costumes and offer free spider juice (apple juice with green food colouring) to the first ten customers.

Hold A Stone-Skimming Contest

All you need to hold a stone-skimming competition is some flat stones and some water, of course. They should not be too light in case they flip over, and not too heavy as you won't be able to throw them properly. Oval-shaped stones work best.

THE TECHNIQUE

Cup the stone with your thumb and forefinger so that they make a C-shape. Your other fingers should be curved underneath the stone.

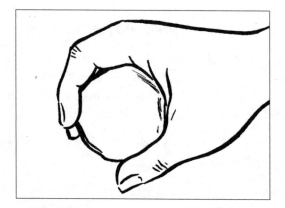

Stand with your legs apart and your knees bent, with one foot leading. If you are holding the stone in your right hand, step forward on your left leg and vice versa.

As you sweep your arm back, try to keep the stone as low and flat as possible (ideally you want the stone to stay nearly parallel to the surface of the water – at an angle of no more than 10 or 20 degrees).

Then jerk the stone forward, using plenty of spin in your wrist and forefinger.

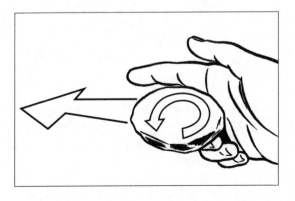

If the stone hits the water front-edge first, it will disappear like a diving duck. If you can, angle the stone so it's almost flat, but with its nose pointing upwards a fraction – this way it is more likely to bounce right across the pond.

WHY THE BOUNCE?

The stone bounces because the surface tension of the water acts like a trampoline. As the stone pushes down, the water pushes upwards.

Did you know?
The world stone-skimming record is held by Russell Byars, called 'Rock Bottom' by his friends, from Pittsburgh, USA. He made a stone bounce 51 times in a single throw.

Put Your Bedroom Underwater

Turn a boring bedroom into an underwater paradise by creating a seabed mural. Instead of waking up in your bedroom, you'll wake to find yourself beneath the Caribbean Sea.

TRANSFORMATION

Using a piece of chalk, draw two horizontal lines that divide your wall from floor to ceiling into three roughly equal bands. Paint the top band (the one nearest the ceiling) sky blue.

When the paint is dry, use your chalk to draw wave crests along the line at the top of your middle band. If the waves go wrong, you can sponge off the chalk and start again.

Using a darker blue than you used for the sky, paint the middle band on your wall, filling in the crests of your waves, too.

Lastly, paint the bottom band (the one just above the floor) yellow to represent the seabed.

Now you can start filling the sea scene with fish. In no time at all you will be surrounded by sharks, electric eels, poisonous jellyfish, and octopuses. Practise them on paper, then sketch your sea creatures on to the wall with chalk before filling them in with different coloured paint. Paint in plenty of colourful coral and tropical fish too, as well as seaweed and brilliant anemones.

Add some pebbles and shells to the seabed. How about some starfish, lobsters and sea urchins with deadly spines that help fend off unwanted visitors?

Make A Tiny Parachute

Make a toy parachute and watch it float to earth. All you need is a circle of cotton fabric 30 cm in diameter and eight pieces of thick thread each about 35 cm long.

Pinch the fabric at a point along the edge of the circle. Tie the end of a length of thread around the gather and knot the string. Tie the dangling end to a small, lightweight toy, such a plastic soldier. Repeat this for each piece of thread at regular intervals around the fabric.

Outside, or where you have space, pinch the centre of the fabric circle and pull it into a thin cone, swing the toy round, then let go, sending it high into the air. As the toy falls, the parachute will open.

Experiment to discover the lowest height that allows the chute to open successfully. Does it work from the bottom of the stairs or when you stand on a chair?

Why not make a parachute for each member of your family and see whose stays in the air longest?

Send A Mysterious Message In A Bottle

Eye-catching decoration is the key to successful bottle-mail. Few people will pick up a tatty-looking bottle, but if it is brilliantly decorated, who could resist? Choose a glass wine bottle with a tight-fitting cork. Why not use enamel paints to create a desert island scene with yellow sand and green palm trees? Alternatively, why not paint 'Open Me!' in multi-coloured letters?

THE MESSAGE

Make the message that goes inside your bottle as imaginative and intriguing as possible, so that the finder replies. Write it as a series of clues describing where the bottle has come from or try composing a poem:

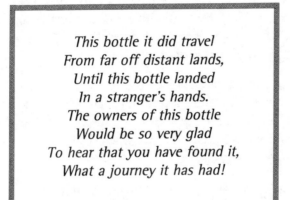

This bottle it did travel
From far off distant lands,
Until this bottle landed
In a stranger's hands.
The owners of this bottle
Would be so very glad
To hear that you have found it,
What a journey it has had!

Use good quality writing paper that won't be destroyed when the bottled is hurled from side to side in the water.

Don't forget to include some contact details, such as an email address, on the back of your message. Never write your telephone number or street address on the message – there is no need to give out such personal information.

IT'S A SEAL

The cork has to be a perfect fit for your bottle. Even a single drop of water could damage your message.

Once corked, seal the bottle by lighting a candle and dripping a thin layer of wax around the cork.

THERE SHE GOES

You want your bottle to travel as far as possible, so ideally, choose a launch point near the open sea. Don't throw the bottle into a bay or a harbour – it won't get very far. If you are throwing the bottle into a stream make sure it is at a point where the river is deep so the bottle won't smash on the riverbed or stones.

The best time to launch your bottle is just after high tide, when the currents are running fast. Throw the bottle as far as possible from the shore or riverbank. Cross your fingers and wait patiently. Who knows where your little vessel will end up, or who will find it.

Warning: Make sure you are not breaking any local littering laws before you send your message in a bottle.

Did you know?
Opening a message in a bottle could get you killed in Elizabethan England. Only the royal 'Uncorker of Ocean Bottles' was allowed to open such bottles, as they often contained messages from spies.

Have A Finger Football Match

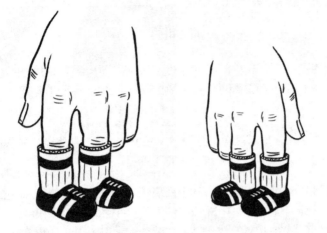

You don't need a stadium that seats 80,000 people and a billionaire owner to play a cracking game of football. A kitchen table, a ping-pong ball and your fingers will do just fine.

Use a piece of chalk to mark out your pitch on a large, flat surface.

Place two open cardboard boxes on their sides to be your goals, or use egg cups for goal posts.

Use your forefinger and middle finger to 'run' across the table and to dribble the ball. You could make boots like the ones shown above with cardboard and papier-mâché, but bare fingers work just as well.

Make sure each team has an equal number of players. Two players can have an excellent match and can play using their left and right hands – one hand playing an attack position, the other staying in defence. This takes practice and it helps if the pitch isn't too large.

THE RULES

• Keep one of your fingers in contact with the ground at all times. Superhuman leaps and 'flying' players are not allowed.

• Take a kick-off from the middle of the table after every goal.

• Corners and penalties are handled in the same way as in a full-sized game. If you grab your opponent's fingers, push or hold them away from the ball, that's a foul and your opponent gets a free kick.

• Your opponent gets a penalty flick if a foul occurs in the goal area.

• Five fouls add up to a yellow card, and two yellow cards mean a sending-off. A sending-off means a player can only use one hand.

• Holding the ball between your fingers, cupping the ball under your palm and using your thumb are all handball offences. Putting one finger on the ball to hold it in place before kicking it away is, however, fair play.

Dowse For Water

The ancient technique of dowsing has been used for thousands of years to search for running water under the ground. The traditional method uses a Y-shaped hazel branch with the dowser holding the tops of the 'Y' and pointing to the ground with the bottom. Use wire coat hangers instead and if you are lucky you might even find a stream running underneath your garden!

Take two wire coat hangers and cut the hook section and one short arm off both hangers so you are left with two L-shaped pieces of wire.

Thread a drinking straw over the shorter arm of each dowsing rod. These are your handles.

Now it's time to start looking for water. Walk at an even pace. Hold the rods, one in each hand, pointing in the direction you are moving. The rods should move around easily in their straw handles. If at any point you walk above an underground river or stream the dowsing rods should cross over one another.

Place a marker in this spot.

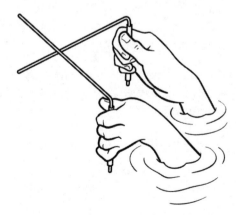

Hand the dowsing rods to someone else and see if the rods react when they walk over the same spot.

Create A Magical Work Of Art

It's time for Dad to use his artistic talents for fun, instead of just painting the living room ceiling. Here's how to create a mesmerizing picture using coloured crayons and black paint.

You will need:

- sheets of thick paper that won't tear easily – the bigger the better • a multi-coloured pack of wax crayons
  - black poster paint and a broad paintbrush
    - newspaper • an old fork

~·~·~·~·~

Using different coloured crayons, decorate a sheet of paper with swirling patterns. Fill every centimetre with whirls and squiggles. Press down hard, and go back over your design. Take a long, loving look at your stunning masterpiece before you cover it up.

Put the sheet on a newspaper and brush black poster paint over it. Slap it on generously, so there isn't a glimpse of colour left.

Now leave the paint to dry.

Test the paint with your fingertip – the effect will be ruined if you start working when it is still wet.

When you are sure it is dry, take the fork and scrape its prongs against the black paint to create one of these spectacular pieces of art:

- magical tigers at midnight

- jewels in an underground cavern

- planets in a distant galaxy

- explorers in their rainbow space rockets

- parrots in the deepest jungle (use dark green poster paint instead of black).

Hold A Gurning Championship

Believe it or not, there's a real art to looking ugly. In fact, there's even a world championship held every year to find the people who can pull the most horrible faces. This skill is called 'gurning', and it dates back hundreds of years.

Take a look in the mirror — have you got what it takes to be a world-champion gurner?

Find someone to act as an impartial judge. Then get gurning.

Disclaimer: The publisher takes no responsibility for the wind changing direction while you've got your gurning face on.

BASIC GURNING

There are three stages to pulling the basic gurning face:

1. Blow your cheeks out.

2. Suck air in through your nose.

3. Open your eyes wide and cross them.

Keep that face for several seconds, but don't freeze it. Make your muscles twitch, your eyes bulge, your neck veins stand out and your ears flap.

The judge then gives marks out of ten for each of these criteria:

- How long you can hold that ghastly look for.
- How much energy and animation shines. through your gurning face.
- How completely your face is transformed by the gurn.

You get a 20 point bonus if you start off good-looking and gurn yourself into a gargoyle.

Did you know?
The World Gurning Championships are held at Egremont Crab Fair in the north-west of England. Competitors put their heads through a horse's harness and do their best gurning face. The fair has been held since 1267.

Some gurners take gurning so seriously that they have teeth removed – to give their face more elasticity. They can achieve stomach-churning effects – like pulling both their lips over their nose – but this is not recommended.

Have Some Egg-cellent Fun

Eggs are much tougher than you think. To prove it, stand over the kitchen sink, and roll up your sleeves. Put an egg in the palm of your hand and close your fingers around it. Try to crush the egg without using your thumb. It's nearly impossible – even for Dad.

A TALL ORDER

You can drop an egg from a height without breaking it – you just need to make sure it lands on grass.

The trick is to make sure the egg lands at an angle, pointed end down, and that it's moving forward at about the same speed as it is falling.

A good way to prove this, if you have a large garden or you can pop along to a park, is to throw an egg as far and as high as you can. As it lands, it should be travelling along as well as down and won't smash, unless of course it hits a tree on its way! Make sure you clear up any eggy mess.

RECORD BREAKING

The world record for dropping an egg from a height without it breaking is held by David Donoghue. In 1994, he threw an ordinary egg out of a helicopter 213 metres above a golf course and retrieved it whole.

PLAY EGG CATCH

To play egg catch, everyone needs an apron or an old raincoat worn backwards.

Find an open, grassy area. Stand three steps from your opponent, and start playing catch with an egg. After two throws, each player takes a step back. Repeat this until you have thrown the egg 20 times. Now you'll be quite far apart, and it will get more and more difficult. The loser is the person who drops or fails to catch the egg and the egg breaks.

If you have four or more players, pair off. Each pair stands opposite each other and throws an egg from one player to the other. After each successful catch, both players take a large step backwards and throw again. See who can make the longest throw without smashing the egg or even getting egg on their opponent's face! You're unlikely to beat the world record set by Keith Thomas and Johnie Dell Foley in 1978 of 98.51 m.

SCRUMMY SCRAMBLED EGGS

If you've still got a few eggs in one piece after the game, why not whip up some delicious scrambled eggs?

For two people you will need:

- 6 eggs • 5 tsps milk
- 1 tbsp butter • salt and pepper to season

Whisk the eggs in a large bowl, then add the milk, salt and pepper. Beat them all together.

Heat a large non-stick saucepan on a medium heat.

Melt the butter in the saucepan, then add the eggy mix.

Turn the heat to low. Once the eggs begin to cook, start scrambling them – moving them backwards and forwards with a wooden spoon, to break them up.

Keep scrambling until the eggs are almost cooked. Then turn off the heat and serve immediately with toast.

A Puzzling Pavement Trick

To see just how low some people will stoop, try this cheeky coin trick.

 Superglue a length of transparent nylon thread to a coin. Be careful not to superglue a finger to the coin in the process. Leave the glue to dry.

Now choose a busy outdoor spot, such as a park or a shopping centre. Find a place where you can position the coin so people will see it, but where you can hide nearby and not be seen.

Hold on to the other end of the thread, making sure the line stays taut. Wait until someone passing by bends to pick up the coin, then quickly tug the coin towards you and away from one very confused passer-by.

Beat The Buzzer

The aim of this game is to guide a wire loop along a length of zigzagging metal without the loop and metal touching and a buzzer going off.

You will need:

• a wire coat hanger • a piece of flat wood approximately 20 cm by 10 cm • an electric doorbell buzzer
• a screwdriver • a 3-volt battery • rubber-coated wire flex • a drinking straw • screws • insulating tape
• a pair of pliers • wire cutters • a drill

Snip the hook off the hanger and open it out. Twist the wire into a series of curves leaving a straight section at each end. Using pliers, bend each end into a tiny C-shape.

Drill a small hole in the wooden base near each end. Put the tip of a screw through each C-shape and screw the wire onto the wood.

Tape a 3-volt battery to the base. Cut a short length of wire flex and strip back the insulation at both ends. Tape one end to the negative terminal of the battery and wrap the other end around one of the buzzer's electrical terminals.

Cut another short length of wire flex and strip back

the plastic on both ends. Wrap one end around the buzzer's other terminal and the other end around the screw at one end of the metal wire.

Slide a straw onto another length of wire flex and strip back 10 cm of the insulation from one end. Bend this into an O-shaped loop around your zigzagging metal wire. Then twist the loop shut without squashing it.

Strip the other end of the wire flex and connect it to the positive terminal of the battery. If the loop touches the wiggly wire it will complete the electrical circuit and set off the buzzer.

IT'S A BUZZ

Take it in turns to hold the straw and guide the loop along the wire without touching it and setting off the buzzer. The winner is the person that gets the furthest along without the buzzer sounding.

Top tip: When you've finished playing, disconnect one of the wires and tape it to the wood so you don't drain the battery.

Make A Cotton-Reel Snake

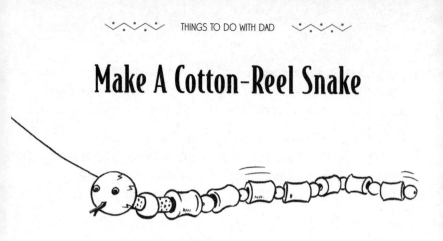

This toy snake slithers like a real snake, but the good news is it won't ever bite.

You will need:

- 7 empty cotton reels
- a string of large beads
- a ping-pong ball • two corks
- a large darning needle and thick cotton
- a small piece of felt • glue • paints
- a hammer and nail

Thread the cotton on to the darning needle and tie a knot at one end. Feed the needle through one of the beads, then through a cotton reel.

Keep threading a bead and then a reel onto the string until all the reels have been used.

Make a hole in each of the corks by carefully hammering a nail into it lengthways then removing the nail. Now add a cork, a bead and another cork to the snake.

Use the needle to make two holes either side of the ping-pong ball. Run the needle through the ping-pong ball to make the snake's head. Then tie off the thread.

Cut out a tab of felt 2 cm long, and snip a V-shape out of one end. This is the snake's forked tongue. Glue the tongue to the head.

Paint eyes and zigzag markings on the ball. Then decorate the reels in snaky colours.

Tie a length of string around the neck of the snake.

Once it has dried, grab hold of your snake and watch it slither.

Have A Thumb-Wrestling Contest

Thumb wrestling might be one of the world's smallest sports, but it requires bags of energy and concentration. In this frantic game, lock hands with an opponent and try to pin down his thumb, without your own thumb getting trapped. The winner is the person who pins down their opponent's thumb the greatest number of times in one game.

RULE OF THUMB

• Before the match starts, agree the number of rounds that will be played. Each round ends when a thumb is pinned down by another thumb for at least four seconds.

• Decide whether forefingers are allowed to wrestle as well as thumbs. It is easier if your forefinger 'snakes' around your opponent's top knuckle to help hold their wriggly thumb, so if you want to keep fingers out of the match, agree on the following pledge:

'No snakes, no buddies and no tag teams.'

This means neither contestant is allowed to move any fingers, just their thumb.

• Remember, this isn't an arm wrestling competition. Your elbows and wrists must not move.

IN THE RING

To make a professional-looking thumb-wrestling ring you will need a piece of sturdy cardboard or light wood.

Cut two holes for the thumbs about 4 cm apart.
If using wood, smooth the edges of the holes with sandpaper to avoid painful splinters.

LET THE GAME BEGIN

Make sure both players understand and agree the rules in advance, so there is less chance of an argument developing.

Sit down at a table, with your chair facing your opponent.

Both players must wrestle using the same hand – right hand to right hand, or left hand to left hand.

Bend the chosen hand to make a curved C-shape without any gaps between your fingers. Keeping your hand in this position, link 'Cs' with your opponent, with the underside of your fingers touching.

Press the tips of your thumbs together and start the game by chanting a rhyme such as:

'One, two, three, four, I declare a thumb war!
Five, six, seven, eight, try to keep your thumb straight.'

Throughout the chant, each contestant repeatedly moves their thumb either side of their opponent's thumb. As soon as the chant has ended, the match begins.

Wriggle, twiddle, bend and twist your thumb to snare the other player's thumb and pin it down for a count of four, chanting *'One, two, three, four, I won the thumb war!'*

Repeat until an agreed number of rounds have been played, or until someone is scared they might dislocate their thumb!

If all else fails, do your best to distract your opponent by making them laugh or lose their concentration. It's totally above board and part of the fun of thumb wrestling.

Top tip: Why not give each thumb a bandanna by tying a tiny strip of different coloured material around its top.

Create A Campfire Classic

You don't have to go far afield to enjoy a night under the stars. Why not set up camp right in your back garden? What is essential, however, is the classic campfire treat – s'mores.

To prepare s'mores, you'll need a campfire, but if you don't want a charred mess in the middle of your lawn, buy a disposable barbecue in a tray at your local supermarket or DIY store.

SUPER S'MORES

You will need:

- a packet of plain biscuits • a large bar of chocolate
- a bag of marshmallows • some metal skewers

Start by making sure your campfire or your barbecue is ready for cooking on. It is best when preparing s'mores to have a fire that is glowing rather than flaming.

Take two biscuits and add a couple of squares of chocolate to one of them.

Pop two marshmallows on to a skewer and hold them just above the flames of the campfire. Keep heating them until the marshmallows are golden brown and deliciously soft. The skewers might get very hot, so make sure you hold them at the end.

Warning: Make sure your marshmallows don't catch fire. If they do, quickly blow them out before they melt and fall off the skewer.

With the marshmallows still on the skewer, place them on top of the chocolate on the biscuit. Then take the other biscuit and make a sandwich. Squeeze the biscuits together as you pull out the skewer – leaving the marshmallows between the biscuits.

Wait until the marshmallows are cool enough to eat before you tuck in.

Delicious. Pass some more s'mores, please!

Have A Welly-Hurling Competition

Welly hurling is an old British game that is still played today. So find an open space well away from roads and houses and toss that boot. How far can you throw a welly?

GIVE IT SOME WELLY

Mark out your throwing line and make sure each competitor stands far enough away from their rivals so they will not be hit by a stray boot.

Decide how many attempts each player gets to achieve their best throw – most people like at least three practice attempts to warm up.

Record each competitor's longest throw by marking the spot where the welly came to rest with a pair of crossed twigs.

If one player wins by a significant distance, introduce a handicap system, by making that person stand further back from the throwing line.

THE MOVES

Underarm or overarm throws are perfectly acceptable, but for best results, hold the Wellington boot by the rim and spin round and round before letting go – think of an Olympic athlete throwing a hammer. Aim to send the welly flying off in an arc, not too low or too high.

WACKY WELLIES

When you've mastered the basic moves, try these variations:

• Try filling your wellies with water before throwing them.

• Apply the 'kick' rule – pull the boot half way onto your foot and see how far you can kick it without falling backwards. Small feet in big boots have the advantage here, because their wellies will fly off easily.

FOOT FUNDRAISER

Welly-hurling competitions are a great way to raise money. If you've got lots of players, at a school fête for instance, use a tent peg to pin a sheet of paper into the ground with the thrower's name on it. Set a low price for three throws and people will be queuing round the field to have a try.

Make A Scarecrow

If you are throwing a party and you want to give it a quirky twist, why not make a scarecrow to welcome your guests? With a sign around his neck and a hand pointing to the fun, he'll bring an instant grin to their faces.

You will need:

• a bamboo pole 3 m long • old clothes
• newspaper or straw (or another type of stuffing)
• a pillowcase • a marker pen
• string • glue • 2 buttons • rubber bands
• a pair of gloves • a sheet of card

Cut the pole into two pieces, one a metre long and the other 2 metres long. Tie the short pole about 50 cm from the end of the long pole to make a cross.

Put a shirt on your scarecrow, using the short pole as his arms, and button it. Knot it at the waist. Stuff the shirt with scrunched up newspaper or anything else that's handy, such as dry leaves. Fill the arms as well as the torso.

Put a jacket over the shirt if you want your scarecrow to look really dapper.

Pull a pair of gloves over the ends of the arms and secure them with rubber bands. Make sure the tip of the pole fits

into a forefinger of one glove so that it can point the way to the party.

Pull one leg of a pair of trousers onto the main pole and up around the stuffed shirt. Use string to tie the trousers securely around the scarecrow's waist, so they stay in place.

Stuff both legs with more newspaper before tying string around the bottom of each leg to keep the stuffing in.

Draw a face on a pillowcase with marker pen. Glue or sew on two buttons for eyes.

Fill the pillowcase with newspaper and tie it onto the pole before adding a hat, scarf and any other items that you fancy.

Now write a welcome message in bright letters on a sheet of card. Tie the card around your scarecrow's neck then stand him by the door or plant him in the garden.

SPOOKY SCARECROW

If you are making your scarecrow to welcome guests to a Halloween party, why not make the head from a pumpkin? Slice off the bottom of the pumpkin and hollow out the insides. Cut out two triangular eyes (with the points facing down), a triangle for the nose, and carve a jagged, toothy grin.

Mount your pumpkin head on the pole.

Warning: Do not put a lit candle anywhere near your scarecrow – particularly not in its pumpkin head. Anything made from newspaper or straw will catch fire before you can say 'spooky'.

Learn The Swimmer's Turn

A 'flip turn' is a fantastic way to speed up your swimming and is guaranteed to make you look seriously cool. Moreover, in a family race this stylish somersault is a great way for younger swimmers to gain a few metres on Dad.

Warning: Practise these somersaults in the middle of the pool, well away from the sides, until you have mastered them. You don't want to bang your head mid-turn.

NOW IT'S YOUR TURN

1. Swim towards the wall of the pool – keep an eye out for it, because you really don't want to head-butt the tiles! (You might like to wear goggles when practising your somersault so that you are able see the wall more clearly.)

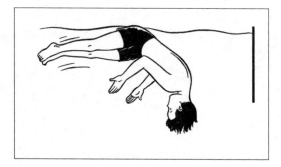

2. When you are an arm's length away from the wall, begin your somersault. Tuck your chin into your chest and scoop your arms towards your feet to propel yourself into the turn.

3. Bend your body forward at the waist. Position your hands either side of your head, with your elbows tucked in. Roll your body into a ball and continue the somersault.

4. Halfway through (when your head is parallel to the floor of the pool again) start to uncurl your body. Straighten your arms, pointing your hands, back towards the centre of the pool. Kick your legs out towards the wall and plant both of your feet firmly against it. Take care not to kick the wall as this will hurt!

5. Using both feet, push off from the wall and propel your body forward through the water. At the same time rotate your body so that you are no longer on your back, but on your front, belly down.

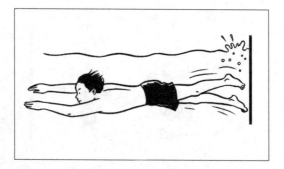

6. Stretch your arms in front of your head and streamline your body like a torpedo. Kick your legs underwater to drive yourself forward and swim up to the surface of the water to take a breath.

Start swimming strongly towards the opposite end of the pool – last one there loses!

Make A Canine Cake

It's easy to forget that dogs have birthdays too. Pets don't want games consoles or DVDs. What matters most to the average mutt is a tasty treat.

Why not make a meaty 'birthday bone' cake from a tin of dog food? You don't even need to use an oven.

Empty a medium-sized tin of chunky, meaty dog food onto an old baking tray.

Divide the contents in two, and mould one half into a flat bar about 15 cm long. If you don't want to touch the meat with your fingers, wear clean rubber gloves.

Break the other half into four pieces and roll them into balls. Flatten these with the heel of your hand, and place two at each end of the 'bone', smoothing out the joins as much as possible.

Open a tin of tuna, drain away the oil or water, and sprinkle it over your dog-food bone as fishy 'icing'.

Slice a carrot into circles and use them to decorate the edges of the bone.

Warning: Chocolate is poisonous to dogs, so don't be tempted to add any to a canine's cake.

Pop some candles on your canine cake and light them – just make sure someone blows the candles out before your pet starts scoffing. You don't want to burn any noses.

If you don't have a dog of your own, make a cake for one of your relative's doting dogs or a neighbour's helpful hound.

CAT CAKE

It is really easy to make a birthday cake for a cat, too. Just mould a small tin of cat food into a semicircle. To make it look like a mouse, add a circle of carrot for an ear, and raisins to make an eye and a nose. For a real treat, add a trail of cream for a tail. That really is the cat's whiskers!

Invent A Secret Handshake

Everyone knows the importance of a firm handshake — not a limp dab of the fingers, but a confident grip, matched with a smile. Secret handshakes are much cooler and can be really way-out – elbows, shoulders and even feet can be involved.

Try these moves, then put some together in a cool combination to make your own family handshake.

- Hook your fingertips together.

- Raise your hands so they are facing the other person and slap each other's palms in a 'high ten'.

- Hold out both hands palms facing upwards to be slapped.

- Wrap both hands around the other person's fist.

- Bump opposite elbows with each other twice.

- Bump opposite shoulders with each other three times.

- Hold your hands together, as if you're praying, then touch your middle fingers to your friend's middle fingers.

- Take it in turns to slap the back of the other person's right hand lightly.

- Link arms and hop around in a circle.

- Jump towards each other and bounce your chests together. (Don't attempt this if Dad has a big belly!)

SHAKE HANDS STREET STYLE

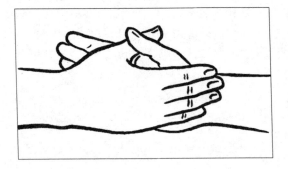

1. Start with an ordinary handshake.

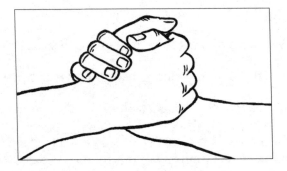

2. Drop your wrist so that your hands twist to a 90-degree angle and hook your thumbs together.

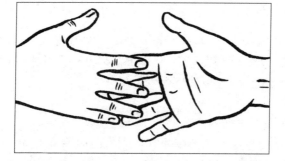

3. Slide your hands apart, wiggling your fingers to tickle each other's palm.

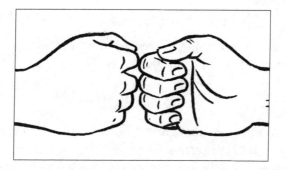

4. Bunch your hand into a fist and rap into the top of the other person's fist twice. Let their fist bounce twice on yours. Then lightly punch your knuckles together.

Build A Water Obstacle Course

You need steady hands and a quick brain to race around an obstacle course carrying a brimming beaker of water.

This is an outdoor game, unless you want to turn your lounge into a swimming pool. You don't need a big space to play it, just a big imagination.

HOW TO PLAY

The race starts at a paddling pool full of water, or a tap, and ends with a row of buckets, one for each player.

Each contestant holds a plastic beaker of water and races around an obstacle course before emptying the water into the bucket. This is repeated ten times. The winner is the player with the most water in their bucket at the end.

To avoid any confusion over whose bucket is whose, label each one with a contestant's name.

THE OBSTACLES

Hunt around your home and garden for objects that can be turned into obstacles. Try some of these challenges and experiment by building your own obstacles and inventing your own moves. (Don't forget to take a beaker of water with you.)

- Walk backwards around the paddling pool.

- Run around a deckchair three times.

- Walk along a plank balanced on bricks.

- Hop back and forth over a bamboo cane four times.

- Do three keepie-uppies with a football (see page 23).

- Add in a star-jump.

- If you are feeling brave and don't mind getting drenched, balance the beaker on your head for three seconds.

Top tips: Make the challenge even harder by not allowing racers to cover their beakers with their hands.

To even up the challenge, give younger players a bigger beaker or a saucepan. Or instead of a bucket, give them an ice cream tub to fill at the end.

Make A Feather Quill

Write like your ancestors did by making a feather quill pen that cannot fail to impress.

You will need:

- a feather about 30 cm long (a turkey or goose feather is best from your local craft shop or an online craft store)
- a tin can filled with sand
- a craft knife • a pot of ink

It is a good idea to get Dad to do the hot and sharp bits of this project. He can create a tailor-made quill pen for each member of the family.

Carefully trim strands or 'tines' of the feather away from the stem until you can hold the stem without being tickled. Medieval scribes would cut all the tines off, but it looks much nicer if some are left at the end.

To make the stem strong, place a can full of sand in an oven at gas mark 4/180°C/350°F for 20 minutes.

Using oven gloves, remove the (very hot) tin can and place it on a heat-proof surface.

Push the tip of the feather deep into the sand and leave it there until the sand cools.

Ask the person whose pen it will be to hold the quill and check the position they feel most comfortable gripping it (usually people like to hold the stem's curve up against their forefinger). Then use the knife to slice the end away, on the underside, by making a 15 mm cut at a shallow angle.

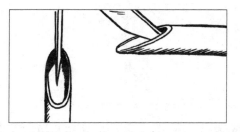

With the point of the knife, split the tip along the middle for 20 mm.

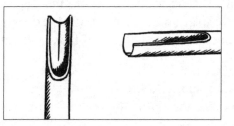

Cut the tip to make it into a crescent shape, like the letter 'C'. This is the trickiest part.

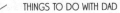

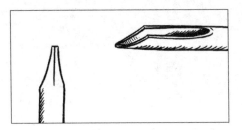

Now shape the nib by making a curving cut either side of the split, to make a sharp tip. Be careful not to cut the nib into too sharp a point.

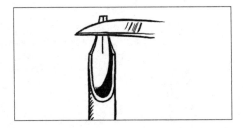

Use the flat of the knife blade to scrape the inside of the tip clean. If the stem is thick, you might want to sharpen the nib from the inside with a tiny cut.

Now it's time to try out your quill. Dip the nib into a pot of ink and get writing. It's trickier than using a ballpoint pen, but your letters will look really great with a little practice.

Top tip: After about 1,000 words, you'll find the nib gets blunt. Just slice the tip of the quill off to make another nib.

Make A Treasure Map

Why not make an ancient treasure map of your garden or local park? Bury some treasure where X marks the spot. Then see if the rest of the family can follow the map.

To make paper look like an ancient sheet of parchment, all you need to do is soak it in cold, strong black tea for about five minutes.

Remove the paper from the tea and spread it out onto a baking tray.

Turn the oven onto the lowest heat. Place the baking tray in the bottom of the oven until the corners of the paper start to curl. Then carefully remove the tray from the oven using oven gloves.

Warning: When it is in the oven, Dad should keep a watchful eye on the map.

For a really authentic effect, use a quill (see pages 94 to 96) to draw your map on the paper. Alternatively, draw your map in pen.

Add some islands and ships and draw a cross to mark where the treasure is hidden.

Shiver me timbers – a real treasure map.

Catch A Shadow

Believe it or not, it really is possible to catch each other's shadow. Here's how...

You will need:

- large sheets of white paper (at least A2)
- a torch • black paper • a pencil
- glue stick • sticky tack • sticky tape • scissors

Use the sticky tack to attach a large piece of white paper to a wall. One person stands sideways to the wall about 60 cm away from the paper. This person is the 'sitter' whose shadow will be caught.

Pull the curtains together to darken the room and shine the torch onto the sitter's profile. Experiment with the distance between the light and the sitter until you get a sharp shadow of their profile that fits on the sheet of paper. The closer you move the torch to the sitter, the larger the shadow or 'silhouette' will be.

Draw around the outline of the silhouette with a pencil. Then take down the paper and cut out the profile.

Tape the paper profile to a sheet of black paper. Using the white cut-out as a template, snip around it again so that have the profile is cut out in black paper.

Finally, use the glue stick to mount the black cut-out onto

a new sheet of white paper. Write your sitter's name and the date at the bottom of the paper.

FREESTYLE SILHOUETTE

In Victorian times, there was a craze for pictures like these. People became skilled at cutting tiny portraits out of paper without even drawing them first. Why not have a go at cutting a profile of each other's faces from a black sheet of paper without drawing the outline? It's more tricky than it sounds.

Did you know?
The silhouette was named after French politician Etienne de Silhouette, who died in 1767. He was a mean, tight-fisted man and people joked he wouldn't waste his money on a painted portrait when he could have a paper cut-out instead.

Play Shove Ha'penny

This game was played as long ago as the 15th century. It was originally known as 'shoffe-groat' or 'slype-groat' after the groat – an old English coin.

You will need:

- a square or rectangular piece of paper (wallpaper is ideal)
  - sticky tape • a piece of board or an old table top
  - a ruler • two felt-tip pens in different colours • coins

SHOVE OFF

Tape the paper smooth-side up to a board or an old table. Fold the end of the paper over the edge of the surface and tape it down securely.

Using a ruler, draw a horizontal line in felt-tip all the way across the paper, about 5 cm down from the top. Now draw a line 5 cm below this line. Keep drawing horizontal lines with the same felt-tip, until you reach the bottom of the paper. The spaces between the lines are known as 'beds'.

Now use the other felt-tip to mark each bed with a point score – low scores for the spaces closest to the players, and high scores at the end furthest away.

Each player has five coins. One at a time they are placed half on and half off the edge of the surface. Then the

player scoots each coin up the board – shoving the edge of the table and the coin with the heel of their hand, or flicking the coin with the tip of their finger.

The object of the game is to land all five coins in a bed and to score the number of points in that bed. A coin straddling a line scores nothing. At the end of each player's turn the coins are cleared away.

THE RULES

• You are allowed to use a coin to nudge another coin on to a bed without it touching any lines. If successful, you score the number of points marked on that bed, as well as any points scored by the new coin.

• When a coin scores, the bed it lands in is marked with a line. Any bed which receives three lines becomes 'dead' and further coins landing in it score no points. When all the spaces are dead, you have reached the end of the game.

Create Your Own Fantastic Fossils

Create your very own dinosaur and footprint fossils.

You will need:

- a plastic dinosaur (shells, twigs and leaves make great fossils too) • a small cup full of cold coffee grounds
- 175 ml of cold water • 210 g of flour • 6 tbsps of salt
  • a baking tray • a sheet of greaseproof paper

Put the cold coffee grounds, flour, salt and water in a bowl and mix together to make a dough. The dough should not be so soft that it sticks to your fingers. If this is the case, add more flour.

Put the greaseproof paper on the baking tray. Break the

dough into small balls and place them on top of the paper. Squash the balls into disks with the palm of your hand.

Turn the toy dinosaur sideways and press it into each disk of dough. Then carefully peel it out to leave perfect dino-imprints.

Bake the fossils at a low heat until they are hard. When they come out they will look delicious, but don't be tempted to eat them!

FOOTPRINT FOSSILS

You will need:

• modelling clay • a hard-boiled egg (in its shell) • a pencil • plaster of Paris • greaseproof paper

Knead the clay and roll it out into a thick, flat disc. Make a raised rim around the edge of the disc by pressing a long sausage-shaped piece of clay around the rim.

Press the bottom of an egg into the clay – then lift it out. The imprint made is the middle of the dinosaur's foot. With your finger make four toe imprints around the foot.

Use a pencil to scratch out a vicious claw at each toe-tip.

Mix a cup of plaster of Paris in a bowl with half a cup of water, and stir it into a soupy paste. Pour the paste into the hollow footprint, making sure there are no air bubbles. Leave to set, then peel the clay away from your footprint.

Harness Balloon Power

Has Dad got enough puff or patience to make a jet-powered toy using a party balloon?

MAKE A MINI JET BOAT

Who needs a real-life speed boat, when you can create a miniature version to race in your bath?

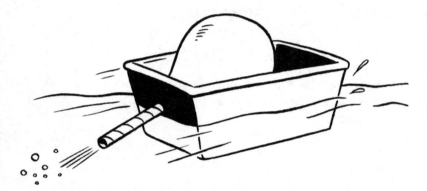

You will need:

- a large margarine tub • a balloon
- the barrel of a ballpoint pen • an elastic band
- a lump of modelling clay • scissors

Start by placing a lump of modelling clay in one end of the margarine tub. This will ensure the boat sits deep in the water instead of bobbing on top.

With the scissors, pierce the end of the tub (the one that is closest to the lump of clay) near the base. Make a hole just big enough to poke the plastic pen barrel through.

Slip the pen barrel through the hole you have made in the tub and into the neck of the balloon. Seal the hole around the pen with more modelling clay. The balloon will be resting inside your tub. Secure it by wrapping the elastic band round and round.

Blow through the pen barrel to inflate the balloon. This takes a lot of puff! When you are finished blowing, hold your finger over the hole at the end of the barrel to stop the air from escaping.

Now put the speedboat in a bathtub or paddling pool and remove your thumb from the hole to set it racing.

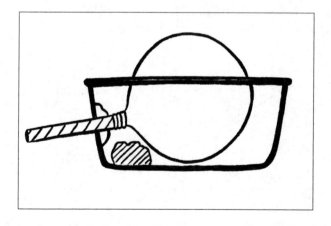

Top tip: Why not make a boat each and see whose boat sails for the longest amount of time? You could even try racing them.

How To Play Achi

This game, which originated in West Africa, is ideal for two people to enjoy. It can be played almost anywhere, but is particularly perfect to play on a lazy day at the beach.

In the sand, mark out the lines of the square board as shown below. Hunt for a collection of pebbles and shells to use as counters – you'll need four of each.

HOW TO PLAY

One person plays using pebbles, the other with shells.

Toss a coin to decide which player starts. Then, taking it in turns, place your counters on the 'board' at any of the points where lines intersect. When all eight counters are in position, players take turns to move their counters into the single empty spot, aiming to be the first player to get three counters in a row.

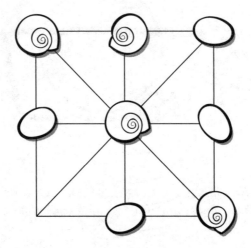

Make A Rainstick

A rainstick is a South American musical instrument made from a cactus filled with hundreds of fragments, such as seeds and small stones. When the stick is turned upside down the seeds make a sound like raindrops falling on leaves. Native South Americans believe this sound encourages the gods to make it rain. Here's how to make a rainstick without a cactus.

You will need:

• cardboard tubes, the sturdier the better
• carpet tacks with flat heads • seeds, beads, lentils, or even pieces of gravel • cardboard • shells and straws to decorate your rainstick • paints • sticky tape

Tape your tubes together to make a long, hollow 'stick'.

Push or hammer carpet tacks into your stick in a spiral pattern stretching from one end of the tube to the other. The more tacks you use, the noisier your rainstick will be, but make sure that the points of the tacks don't stick through the other side of the stick.

Cut a circle of cardboard, and tape it over one end of the stick to seal it. Now pour in handfuls of seeds, lentils, gravel and beads. Seal the other end with another circle of cardboard to make sure the contents will not fall out all over the floor, making you unpopular with Mum.

Paint your rainstick with bright tropical colours. Why not add shell patterns and some feathers cut from coloured paper?

For the best effect, don't shake the rainstick. Simply turn it on one end and let the contents trickle through the spikes. Then turn it over again, like an egg timer. Wait and see if it rains!

Get 'Tuned In'

'Tuned in' is a game that costs absolutely nothing to play. All you need is a radio, a timer or stopwatch, and some paper and pens.

HOW TO PLAY

Each player takes it in turns to tune the radio to a random channel and leaves it there for 10 seconds. That player scores points depending on what is being broadcast on the channel they have selected. The winner is the person who scores the most points in one hour.

Top tip: You might also like to keep a blindfold handy to stop players peeking at the frequency of the radio as they turn the dial or change the channel.

This table shows the points awarded for each subject the radio might be playing. If there is an overlap of subjects during those 10 seconds, it is the first subject that counts.

• Music: 1 point
Bonus: An extra 3 points if you can name the song or piece of music and 5 more if you can sing or hum the next line

• News: 2 points
Bonus: 5 extra points if the player can explain what the news story is about

• Foreign Language: 3 points
Bonus: An extra 3 points if you can name the language

• Adverts: 3 points
Bonus: 5 points if you've ever bought the product

• Classical Music: 4 points

• A Jingle: 5 points
Bonus: 10 points for singing the whole jingle yourself

• A Weather Report: 5 points

• Sports Match: 5 points

• Phone-in: 5 points
Bonus: 10 extra points if you can give an instant opinion on the topic

• Traffic Report: 5 points

Once you've learned how to play the basic version of 'Tuned In', try these variations:

Radio Bingo: Each player has their own piece of paper with a list of all of the categories shown opposite. When a player tunes into one of the categories they can cross it off their list.

The winner is the first person to cross off each of the categories. They can then shout: *'I'm tuned in!'*

In A Spin: Before play begins, draw a large circle on a piece of A4 paper, and divide it into ten segments.

Write the name of one category in each of the sections.

Then using a pen as a spinner, one player spins to select the 'instant loser' category.

Now, wearing a blindfold, take it in turns to choose a channel. If a player chooses a station that is broadcasting the instant loser programme they are automatically out of the game.

Continue until only one person remains.

Make A Button Yo-Yo

You can create a nifty, personalised yo-yo with just two large coat buttons (look for two that are at least 2 cm wide) and some extra-strong thread.

Cut 50 cm of thread and, holding the buttons back to back, lace the thread back and forth between all of the holes. Keep going until the buttons are securely tied together with a slight gap between them.

Push the thread through one of the holes and pull it out between the two buttons. Loop it three times around the cotton core, then knot it securely on itself.

Tie a loop in the other end of the thread that is large enough for you slip your middle finger through. If you are right-handed use the middle finger of your right hand.

Wind the thread of your yo-yo around the core until it is wound all the way up to the loop and you can hold the yo-yo in your palm.

LET'S GO AND YO-YO

Flip your fingers down and let the yo-yo roll off them. As it falls, turn your hand over, jerk the thread and snatch the yo-yo as it comes back up.

Breathtaking Ball Spinning

Find out who can master this brilliant ball trick first, and who can achieve the longest spin.

Place the ball on your upturned palm, with your arm extended and slightly bent at the elbow. Practise flicking the ball about 6 cm into the air with a pat of your hand. Try putting some spin on the ball by rotating your wrist with an anti-clockwise flick if you are right-handed. (If you are left-handed, rotate your wrist clockwise.)

When you can do this confidently, as the ball leaves your hand, point your index finger up and let the ball land directly onto it. (Practise so you make contact at the centre of the ball.) The more spin you put on the ball as it goes up, the faster and longer it will spin.

If you're getting really good, try flicking it up from your fingertip to increase the spin and catching it again. Do this correctly and the ball will look weightless.

Cook Up Some Spooky Food

Whether it's Halloween or just a boring day that needs spooking up, conjure up these ghoulish dishes.

MONSTER'S EGGS

You will need:

- 6 cooking apples
- a handful of raspberries or blueberries
- squirty whipped cream
- a scoop of butter • brown sugar • maple syrup
- an apple corer • kitchen tongs

Preheat the oven to Gas Mark 4/180°C/350°F. Then wash the apples and remove the cores with an apple corer.

Place the apples in an oven-proof dish and tip ½ cm of boiling water into the dish.

Pour several teaspoonfuls of sugar into the hole in the middle of the apples and seal them with a knob of butter.

Cook the apples for about 35 to 40 minutes before removing them. They should be soft but not collapsing. Now transfer them to a tray using the tongs. Be careful not burn yourself.

Here's the fun bit. Trickle a spoonful of maple syrup over the top of the apples. Then squirt whipped cream into the centre of each one. The cream will swell up and ooze over the top like something from a horror movie, and that's when you scatter the berries over the bubbling cream.

Now shriek, '*Aaarghh. They're hatching!*' and serve!

Top tip: To create some creepy cracks in the eggs, Dad can make some vertical cuts a few centimetres into the sides of the apples when they come out of the oven.

HANDS OF THE UNDEAD

All you need for this is some jelly, a pair of rubber gloves and an elastic band.

 Mix up a bowl of jelly using the method suggested on the packet. Lime jelly is a good choice.

Wash the gloves inside and out. Then carefully hold each glove at the wrist with the fingers pointing down and pour in the jelly.

Tightly tie the tops of each glove with rubber bands. Now place each hand in the freezer. Leave them overnight so that they freeze solid.

Now take the frozen hands out of the freezer and run them under a cold tap for a few seconds.

 Slowly remove the gloves by using scissors to cut the wrist of the gloves away from the jelly.

When the hands are free at the wrists, slowly cut away the fingers of the glove, being very careful not to snap the icy fingers off.

Put the hands in the fridge to defrost. When they are soft enough to eat, grab some spoons and tuck in.

The Cream-Cracker Challenge

Challenge each other to the ultimate snacking test. All you need are three cream crackers and a stopwatch, plus a lot of will and determination. Dad might be able to eat more food in one sitting than anyone else in the family, but will he be able to take this cracking challenge?

Face each other with three cream crackers per person close at hand. Stare into your opponent's eyes to try to freak them out before you start.

THE RULES

- Players are up against the clock, with just one minute to consume all three crackers.

- Contestants are not allowed to drink any water during their minute, but they can have a glass at hand for their recovery.

WATER, WATER!

It might not look like a lot of food to chomp on – the first cracker might seem super-easy and be on its way to your stomach in moments – but just see how the second and third go down.

Most people will find that their mouths simply can't produce enough saliva to allow them to swallow all three dry crackers.

Give it a try – you'll need that glass of water.

Make An Underwater Viewer

Wouldn't it be great to see more clearly into ponds and rockpools? Here's a simple viewer you can make to explore underwater.

You will need:

• a stiff cardboard tube that is open at both ends • a sheet of acetate • duct tape • a craft knife

Using a sharp craft knife, cut a circle of acetate that fits snugly over one end of your tube – like the lens of a telescope.

Wrap a strip of duct tape around the end of the tube, overlapping the acetate slightly. Fold it down over the edge of the acetate to secure it. Keep adding tape until you are confident that your telescope is watertight.

Next, wrap duct tape up and over the whole of your tube to waterproof it.

When you hold the open end of the tube up to your eye, you should be able to see through it clearly.

Now take your telescope on a rock-pooling or pond-life expedition and see what you can spot.

Submerge the acetate end of your viewer. Move it around slowly so as not to scare away the wildlife you are watching. If the water isn't too murky, you'll be able to see well.

Top tip: Why not draw up a list of things that you should be able to spot in the pool or pond you are exploring? The first player to cross off everything on their list shouts '*Bingo!*'.

Make A Dancing Puppet

Ever heard of a monkey-nut boy band or peanut puppet show? Here's how to make a seriously strange puppet.

You will need:

- a bag of monkey nuts (peanuts, still in their shells)
- 2 ice lolly sticks • a long darning needle • a reel of strong thread • paint and brushes
- a thimble

⋋·⋋·⋋·⋋·⋋·⋋·⋋

Start by threading the nuts together to make your dancing puppet. You need to thread a 70 cm length of strong thread through the needle. Use it double thickness to make it stronger. Tie a fat knot 4 cm from one end and, using a thimble, push the needle right through one nut lengthways (the belly of your puppet) from bottom to top. Tie a knot above the nut to keep it in place.

Make another knot ½ cm above the body. Thread a second nut on to your needle to make your puppet's head. Knot the thread above the nut, and leave the long end trailing.

Using another length of thread, push the needle through the back of the body nut at the shoulder and out to the side where the arm will start. Thread on two nuts and repeat on the other side.

Tie a knot before and after each nut, always leaving a slight gap. Leave the long ends trailing.

Repeat this process to make the legs, but use 90 cm lengths of thread double thickness. Leave the thread at the end of each leg hanging.

Bind the lolly sticks together with thread to make a cross-shape. Attach the head to the middle of the cross.

Attach each arm to different ends of one lolly stick and each leg to different ends of the other.

Use paints to create your puppet's costume, and give him, or her, a cheerful face. Why not make a Wild West bandit with a scowl and a drooping wool moustache?

Now practise making your puppet pal kick and whirl.

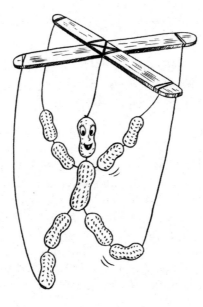

Put On A Magic Show

Stage a magic show for your family and friends and you'll have them gasping in awe at your magical powers. The great thing is that you can take it in turns to be the magician, or the magician's assistant. Just make sure you practise the tricks thoroughly before you perform them in front of your audience. You don't want to be booed off stage!

MYSTICAL MAGIC EIGHTS

Here's a great card trick which will convince your audience you can read minds. You need any seven playing cards and the eight of clubs, a blindfold and the help of a volunteer from the audience who doesn't know how the trick works.

Decide which of you will be the magician and which the magician's assistant.

The magician deals out the eight cards, face up on a table, so that they are arranged in the same pattern as the eight clubs on the eight of clubs card.

Then the assistant ties a blindfold over the magician's eyes.

The assistant asks for a volunteer from the audience and invites them to come up and select one of the eight cards, and show it to the audience. The volunteer then puts the card back in its place. All this is done in complete silence so the magician cannot possibly guess the card.

The magician removes the blindfold. The assistant points, seemingly at random, to the cards on the table. When the assistant points at the volunteer's chosen card, the magician shouts, '*I feel a strong vibe telling me that is your card*' – and it is!

WHAT'S THE SECRET?

To make this trick work, the assistant indicates to the magician which card was chosen in a very simple way. Before pointing to the chosen card, the assistant points a finger at the eight of clubs. He or she carefully only touches one of the clubs on the face of the card. The one touched corresponds to the position of the chosen card in the layout of the eight cards. For example, if the ace was the chosen card, the magician would point to the club circled below on the eight of clubs.

A CRAFTY CARD TRICK

For the next trick, reverse roles – so that the magician is now the assistant and the assistant the magician.

The magician holds a pack of cards face down and shows the audience what they think is the card on the top of the pack.

Instead of lifting just the top card, the magician picks up the first and second card in one go – hiding the top card behind the second. (It is easier to lift the two cards in one go if, before the performance, you have bent them slightly – in private, practise lifting the cards smoothly and confidently.)

After the magician has shown the audience what is in fact the second card, he or she replaces both cards on top of the pack.

The magician holds out the deck of cards and the assistant takes the top card and slips it into the middle of the pack while telling the audience: 'I am placing the top card in the middle of the pack.'

The card that the audience was shown is now on the top of the pack.

The magician taps the pack and says 'Abracadabra!'

The magician's assistant then shows the audience the top card and they marvel in amazement, believing the card that they saw placed in the middle of the pack has magically returned to the top.

Create A Magic Wheel

Back in Victorian times, there weren't any DVDs or computer games. A 'zoetrope', or 'magic wheel', was the nearest thing to TV. Here's how to make one of your own.

You will need:

- a piece of cardboard (25 cm by 25 cm)
- a large sheet of coloured paper (at least 70 cm by 22 cm)
- a strip of white paper (70 cm by 6 cm)
- felt-tip pens • two 30 cm-long dowelling rods
- a ruler • sticky tape • glue • a pair of scissors
- a pair of compasses • a piece of string 2 m long

∿·∿·∿·∿·∿·∿

Use a pair of compasses to draw a circle on the cardboard 21 cm in diameter. Cut the circle out.

Take the coloured paper and cut three strips 70 cm in length. Make one strip 5 cm wide, one 7 cm wide and one 10 cm wide.

Take the 10 cm-wide strip and cut it into 15 sections – each 4 cm wide. Firmly glue the short edges of the strips along the length of the 7 cm-wide strip, leaving a gap of a ½ cm between each strip. You should have a short gap at the end.

Now take the 5 cm-wide strip, and glue it securely along the top of the sections. This will be your viewing wheel.

With the 7 cm strip at the bottom, cut 1 cm notches along the lower edge. Curve your viewing wheel around the cardboard circle, folding the notches over. Use tape and glue 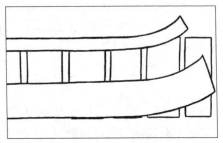 to fix the circle in place. You will also need to tape the top strip to complete the cylinder.

Take the strip of white paper that is 70 cm by 6 cm. This will make your movie sequence strip.

Draw 15 figures, evenly spaced along the strip. Make each picture slightly different – if you were showing a man running, his arms  and legs would be in a slightly different position in each picture. Slide this picture strip inside the slatted frame and push it back against the frame so it runs all the way round, like wallpaper.

Pierce two holes, opposite each other, in the top of the paper frame and slide one of the dowelling rods through both holes. Do the same with the other rod, fractionally lower and at right angles to the first. The two rods will form a cross in the middle.

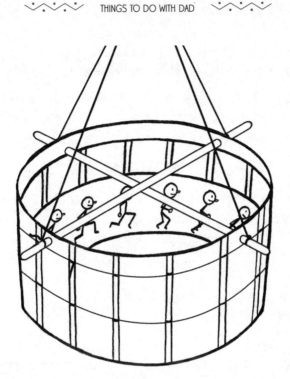

Cut four lengths of string, 50 cm each. Tie a piece to each end of the dowelling rods. Bring the four ends to the middle of the wheel and tie them together.

Suspend the magic wheel by holding the ends of the string in one hand. Now twist the wheel in the opposite direction to the running character. Let go of the wheel and peep through the slats as it spins. Watch as your little figure comes to life! Now spin the wheel in the opposite direction so the character runs backwards and the strings untangle.

Alternative ideas for animations that will work well in your zoetrope are jumping fish and bouncing balls. Keep your sequences simple for the best result.

Become A Knight

Knights of old proudly wore their family's coat of arms on their shield during jousting matches. Here's how to create some bunting that includes your own family's coat of arms.

You will need:

- a piece of white card at least 40 cm by 50 cm
- large sheets of coloured paper in at least two colours
- string • felt-tip pens • masking tape • glue
- a ruler • scissors

～·～·～·～·～

Draw a shield shape on to the white card, 35 cm wide and 45 cm long. Use a ruler to draw two lines 5 cm apart across the middle of the shield. Start the first line about 20 cm down from the top.

Now use a pair of scissors to cut out your shield.

SYMBOLS OF THE KNIGHT

 Dream up two designs that symbolise your family. For example, if your surname is Smith, you could draw a horseshoe in the top half of the shield. If it is Mann, you could draw a man. If there's an artist in the family, you could try drawing a palette with a brush, or you could use Dad's occupation for inspiration.

For the bottom half of the shield, choose a design inspired by an activity you enjoy together. For example, draw waves if you love visiting the beach, a cricket bat or football if you are sports fans, or a castle if you love visiting historic places.

To finish off your coat of arms, shade the three sections of the shield in different colours. How about red in the top section, green at the bottom and yellow in the stripe?

Measure a length of string that will span the room you want to hang the bunting across. Cut it just long enough so that it hangs down in a gentle arc. Pierce a hole in the top two corners of your shield and thread the shield onto the string, pulling it into the middle.

TIME TO ADD SOME BUNTING

No knight's debut would be complete without lashings of multi-coloured bunting.

Take some sheets of coloured paper that match the colours on your shield and cut them into strips, 30 cm by 15 cm.

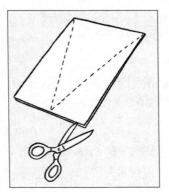

Fold the strips in half lengthways and cut a V-shape from the open base to form a pennant. Repeat with different colours of paper.

Open out the folded shapes and put a thin line of glue on the inside of the folds before gluing the pennants on to your string.

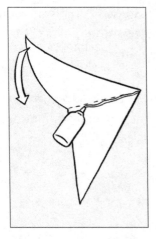

Add more pennants side-by-side along your bunting until the string is full. Then hang it across the room, securing the ends with masking tape.

Congratulations. You have been knighted!

Grow Your Name In Cress

Every year, parks and stately homes spend huge amounts of money on elaborate floral displays. Primroses and pansies are planted in the shape of mermaids, whales and ships. Some towns use flowers to spell out their names across flowerbeds. It's time to achieve the same effect for your family – albeit on a smaller scale – by writing your names in cress.

You will need:

• a packet of cress seeds • an old hand towel
• a sheet of paper • plastic wrap • a baking tray

Wet the towel with warm water, so that it's damp but not soaking wet. Lay it flat in the tray.

Fold your sheet of paper in half and sprinkle seeds along the fold so it is easy to pour the seeds accurately.

Tipping the paper carefully, pour a stream of seeds on to the towel, spelling out your name. If your name is super-long you could just do your initials or nickname, otherwise you will need to find a beach towel!

Cover the tray with a length of plastic wrap and seal it around the edges.

Place the tray somewhere warm where it can get a little sunlight, and leave it there for two days. Then uncover the towel and water it slightly.

Leave the towel uncovered and place it in a really sunny spot (but not glaring sunlight). The cress will begin to grow – don't forget to water it now and again.

Make the most of your crop by harvesting it and serving it in a sandwich with a sliced hard-boiled egg!

Create Your Own Solar System

Here's your chance to create a whole solar system of your own – one that's tiny enough to fit in your house!

You will need:

- 5 tennis balls • 5 ping-pong balls
- poster paints and brushes • duct tape
- eye hooks • a sheet of white card
- three 1 metre-long wooden sticks
- a ball of wool • a long darning needle
- a craft knife

Get to work with your paints to transform the tennis balls into planets. Paint them different colours – one could have swirls of red to show electrical storms battering the planet. One could have clouds and continents. Go crazy – it's your solar system.

Why not cut out a ring of card and push it over one of the balls to represent rings (like those that circle Saturn in our own solar system)? Secure the card with duct tape and spatter the ball and the ring with paint dots.

Paint one tennis ball bright orange, because this will be the star at the centre of your solar system.

Now make some smaller planets from the ping-pong balls.

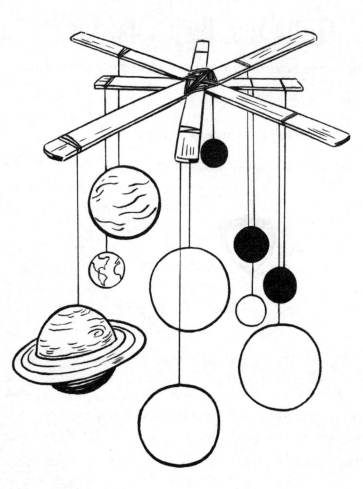

Again, paint them exactly as you like, making each one different.

GET MOBILE

 To make the frame of your mobile, cut one of the metre-long sticks in half.

Then use some wool to bind the two 50 cm lengths together – into the shape of a cross.

Make another cross using the other metre-long stick.

Then bind the two crosses together into an eight-pointed star (as shown in the picture opposite). This is the frame on which your solar system will be suspended.

Next, you need to attach the planets to the frame. Thread a length of wool through a long darning needle and tie a big knot in the end. Push the needle through a ping-pong ball and tie it to one of the sticks. Repeat for the other four ping-pong balls.

To add the tennis balls to your frame, screw an eye hook into each ball. Attach a length of wool to each eye hook and suspend the tennis balls from the sticks of your frame.

Hang the fifth orange tennis ball that is your star from the middle of the mobile's frame, where the sticks cross. This star forms the centre of your solar system – like the Sun sits at the centre of our solar system.

Hang your mobile from the ceiling and push the planets around until the whole structure balances. Then stand back and admire your creation.

Your Five Minutes Of Fame

Why not play a great game called 'Botticelli'? It is perfect for two or more players and will bring a touch of star quality to long, boring journeys.

For each round, one person is the chooser and the rest are questioners. The chooser thinks of a famous person (be fair, make sure it is one that all players will have heard of). The chooser then tells the other players the first letter of the celebrity's surname. For example, if the chooser picked George Bush, they would announce that the surname began with the letter 'B'.

Now the other players have to think of a famous person whose surname begins with the right letter. One questioner might guess that the celebrity was David Beckham, another might guess Gordon Brown.

The player sitting on the right hand of the chooser takes the first turn, and asks the chooser a question to find out if they are right in their guess. They might ask '*Are you a British footballer who now plays in the USA?*'

The chooser must try to work out who the questioner is thinking of. He might say '*No, I'm not David Beckham.*' If the chooser has guessed correctly, it is the next player on his right's turn to ask a question. However, if the chooser fails to guess correctly, the questioner reveals the name of their celebrity. In return, they get to ask the chooser a direct question, such as '*Are you male?*' The chooser can only answer '*yes*' or '*no*'.

Each time the answer is '*yes*', the guesser is allowed to ask

another question, until they can guess the identity of the celebrity or until they ask a question that receives the answer '*no*'.

If a guesser thinks they know the identity of the chooser's celebrity they must ask a question – for example, '*Are you George Bush?*'

The person who guesses correctly is the chooser in the next round.

WHY BOTTICELLI?

This game is named after Sandro Botticelli because, as a rule of thumb, the stars that players choose should never be more obscure than him. You may well ask – who was Sandro Botticelli? Well, he was an Italian painter, but this demonstrates that choosers should only pick well-known celebrities about whom they know something.

Marble Madness

People have been playing marbles for centuries – even before Dad was a boy.

The best known method of 'shooting' a marble is a technique called 'fulking'. Bend your index finger into a U-shape and place the second knuckle on the ground. Rest a marble in the U-shape of the bent index finger. Use your thumb to flick the marble off your finger.

Here are some great marble games.

MONEY MARKSMAN

One player places a marble on a coin. The other players attempt to knock it off. Those who miss lose their marbles. The player who manages it wins the coin!

SPANNERS

One player shoots a marble along the ground. The second player then shoots a marble, and it must land within a hand's span of the first marble. If they are successful, they pocket the first marble and the game begins again, with the winner as the placer. If they miss, a third player takes a turn trying to put a marble within a hand's span of the second shot, and pockets all the marbles if successful.

THREE HOLES

Find a flat area of earth without any grass. Scoop out three holes in the ground using a sharp stone, stick or trowel. Players take it in turn to try to land marbles in all three holes, one after the other. If a marble hits another marble and shunts it into a hole, that still counts as 'on-target'.

The first player to hole three marbles in three shots wins.

LAG OUT

Place a marble near a wall. Players take turns bouncing marbles off the wall, trying to hit the placed marble. As players fail, there will be more marbles to hit.

Any player who hits a marble can retrieve their marble and choose one other. Keep playing until someone has won all the marbles or all the marbles are on the ground and nobody has won.

Hold A Golden Goal Competition

Hold your very own golden goal competition to see who can score the most penalties with ten attempts.

Ideally, pop to a park nearby that has a football pitch and a goal. Failing that, draw a rectangle to act as your goal on an outside wall with chalk (choose an area of wall well away from windows). If you are not playing on grass it is a good idea to put down a mat in front of the goal to prevent injuries to your goalie.

Draw a penalty spot on the floor about 7 m in front of the middle of the goal mouth.

Choose someone to be the goalkeeper and someone to be the ball-bending penalty shooter. You will also need a third person to act as a referee.

When a penalty is taken, the goalkeeper must remain on the goal-line between the posts until the ball is kicked by the shooter. The keeper can jump up and down, wave their arms, and move from side to side along the goal line – attempting to distract the shooter.

The shooter must outwit the goalie and get the ball into the net with one kick. Here are some tips on how to score a penalty:

- Place the ball on the spot. Then tread down any loose turf that might affect your kick.

- Make a decision about where to aim the ball, but don't give the goalkeeper any clues (either with your eyes or your body language) as to which area of the goal you are aiming for. The corners marked below are the best bits of the goal to aim for.

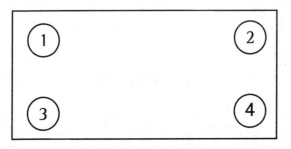

- You need a short run-up to make sure that you have the maximum power behind your kick, so step six paces back from the ball.

- Wait for the referee's whistle, then approach the ball at an angle and boot it into your chosen corner.

- Goal!

Car Wash Party

If you want to raise funds and have some foamy fun at the same time, why not have a car wash party?

You will need:

• a hose • a bottle of soap suitable for washing cars
• a bucket and 2 sponges for each car washer

SPREAD THE WORD

Let your neighbours know at least a week in advance when you will be holding your car wash party. Weekends are best, since most people take their cars to work on weekdays. Why not make some flyers to put through letter boxes?

SHOW ME THE MONEY

Set a price beforehand for each full car wash. Don't undersell yourself. Find out what the local mechanical car wash costs and charge just under this amount – you are saving your customers time and trouble, after all.

ON TAP

Delegate one person to shuttle between the front door and the hot taps with buckets. For cold water, it's best if you can get to a tap without traipsing back and forth through your house. Use a hose attached to an outdoor tap if you have one.

Make sure you all wear old clothes and wellies to this party.

Now it's time to knock on doors and offer your car washing services. Ask your customers to park their cars on the road or driveway where your hose can reach them.

WASH TIME

To get a car really clean, sluice it down with cold water first. Then wash it in sections with hot, soapy sponges. Start with the roof, then the windscreen and bonnet, before tackling the back, the sides and, finally, wheel arches and the wheels.

Get the sponges sopping wet, and rinse them through frequently. Try not to waste water or use more water than is necessary, but change the water when it becomes really dirty, or you will end up scraping dirty sponges over the bodywork, and that creates scratches.

HANDY HINTS

- As you finish each section, rinse it off with cold water.
- Always wash from the top down, so that muddy water isn't dripping over clean panels.
- Use your sponge in long, straight strokes – a circular motion can cause swirls on the paintwork.
- Don't use washing-up liquid on cars as this can damage the paintwork.
- Use a different sponge and bucket for the wheels to avoid picking up grit from the brake pads.

- One person should stay on hose duty while the others wash. Keep switching people round so that each person takes a turn with the hose.

When you have finished your washing bonanza count out the money you have earned and share it equally between each person. If the party has been a success, why not make it a yearly event?

COMPETITION TIME

If the party is big enough, split into two teams and hold a race to see who can wash a car faster. Award bonus points for a super-clean finish.

Build A Teepee

Instead of putting that boring old tent up in the garden again, impress your friends and neighbours by building a Sioux teepee. Take turns to be chief!

You will need:

- a dozen bamboo canes about 2 m long
- strong twine • old sheets or blankets • a stepladder
- safety pins • clothes pegs

Take three canes and lay them on the ground. Knot twine around the top of the canes to tie them into a tripod.

Lift up the tripod and push the canes apart to balance it. Lean the other canes around the tripod, spacing them evenly.

Using a stepladder to reach, tie all your canes together at the top with twine.

Now arrange the canes to form a circular base approximately 2½ m in diameter. Widen the gap between two canes to act as a doorway.

Grab your blankets or sheets and start pegging them to the canes. Start at the bottom of the teepee, and work your way to the top. Don't forget to leave a gap for the entrance.

Use safety pins to hang a strip of the cloth across your entrance.

Now you are ready to have a powwow in your teepee. Why not make up a sign language to communicate with each other?

Friends

Hold out one arm with the hand open.

Cross both arms and shiver.

Winter

Our Tribe

Thump your chest above your heart with a clenched fist.

Make A Swirler Whirler

In the 18th century, before computer games were even invented, this simple toy kept people occupied for hours. What are you waiting for? Give it a whirl.

You will need:

- stiff white card • colouring pens
- elastic thread (about 60 cm long)
- a large jam jar lid • scissors

Place the jam jar lid on the card. Draw around it twice to make two separate circles and cut them out.

Decorate one side of each circle with bold patterns. You could divide one into different coloured quarters and the other into coloured stripes.

With the tip of a pair of scissors, gently poke two small holes in each circle about 1 cm either side of the central point. The holes should be just big enough to thread the elastic thread through.

Place the two circles, plain sides together.

Then thread the elastic one way through both circles, loop around, then pass one way back through both circles. Tie the two ends of the elastic together.

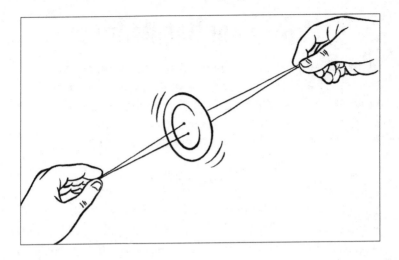

Tuck your middle fingers through each loop of elastic. Then, using your thumbs and index fingers, twist the disks so they rotate away from you, over and over, until the elastic is taut. This can be awkward, but you will soon get the knack.

Finally, pull both loops outwards, so that the elastic untwists and the disks spin. Maintain the spin by moving your hands in and out – increasing and decreasing the tension on the elastic. Watch as the patterns you have drawn distort.

You can experiment by drawing different patterns on the disks to see what they look like when they swirl. Try hearts, spots, stars and zigzags.

Brilliant Bagatelle

'Bagatelle' is a game in which players release marbles at the top of a board, and watch as they bounce off rubber bands and nails. The balls land in the pockets at the bottom of the board to score points. Make your own bagatelle board and watch those marbles bounce.

You will need:

- a sheet of plywood approximately 50 cm by 30 cm
- three lengths of wood for the sides (two 50 cm long and one 30 cm long) • a block of wood 10 cm by 10 cm by 10 cm • 4 large matchboxes (wide enough for a marble to roll through) • a box of small nails • a packet of rubber bands (various sizes) • five marbles
- a hammer • glue • a felt-tip pen

Start by nailing the three lengths of wood that will act as the sides of your board to the plywood base. Leave one of the short ends open.

Remove the outer sleeve from the four matchboxes. Cut one of the top faces of each sleeve off, then glue all the three-sided sleeves in a row at the top of the board.

Next, cut the front off each of the matchbox trays. Glue them side-by-side along the bottom of the board (with the open end pointing towards the top of the board), so they form 'pockets' for marbles to roll into.

With a felt-tip pen mark each tray with a number between one and four to show the number of points scored when a marble lands in that pocket.

Next, hammer small nails all over the table. Stretch rubber bands between some of the nails as shown in the picture below.

Use a block of wood to prop up the top end of the board (the one with the matchbox sleeves attached) so that the board tilts (the taller the block, the more the board tilts and the faster the marbles travel).

PLAYTIME

Launch a marble by rolling it through a sleeve at the top of the board. Watch it ping off the bands and nails until it winds up in a pocket. If it doesn't bounce and ping enough add more bands and nails.

Total what each player scores
with their five marbles.
The highest score wins.

Have A Bubble Party

Why not have a bubble-blowing competition – the bigger the bubbles the better? Here are some tips on how to make the best bubbles ever.

THE PERFECT MIX

For a great bubble mixture, add eight tablespoons of washing up liquid and four tablespoons of glycerin (available from any pharmacist) to a litre of water. Leave the mixture to stand overnight.

For extra effect, add a few drops of food-colouring into the mix – but head outside if you do this, as it gets messy!

A GIANT BUBBLE MAKER

Pour your bubble mix into a large, shallow tray.

Thread two straws onto a metre length of string. Tie the string in a loop between the two straws.

Holding a straw in each hand as handles, dip the loop into your bubble mix, then gently lift it out. You should have a shimmering film of bubble mix in the middle of your loop.

Hold one arm above the other and spin your whole body around in a slow circle. The mixture in the loop should billow out into a bubble.

Try twisting the straws to bring the two sides of the loop together, allowing the bubble to float free.

Top tip: As you get better at this bubble-making method, increase the length of the string – Dad could try a piece 3 m long.

Compete to see who can make the biggest bubble, who can make a bubble last the longest and who can catch a bubble without bursting it.

BUBBLE PIPE

To make a bubble pipe, use the tip of a ballpoint pen to make a small hole near the base of a polystyrene cup.

Insert the short end of a bendy straw into the hole and point the end up towards the top of the cup.

Fill the cup with enough bubble mix to cover the tip of the

straw. Holding the other end of the straw level with the top of the cup, blow gently into the straw and the liquid will start to foam and bubble.

Make Paper Helicopters

Imagine having your very own helicopter that is easy to land and does not have any complicated controls. See who can make the best helicopter that spins the fastest.

WHIRLY BIRD

To make one, cut a strip of paper 3 cm by 12 cm. Make a cut, a centimetre deep, at the midpoint of each long side.

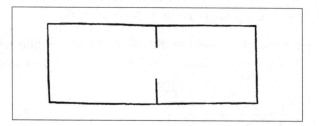

Now score a line from the bottom of each cut along the left-hand side of the cut to the edge of the paper.

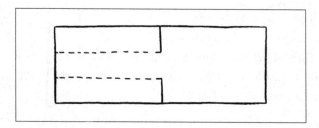

Fold the bottom section up along the score line and then fold the top section down as shown below.

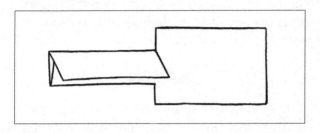

Now the left-hand side of the strip is triple thickness and 1 cm wide. Slip a paperclip over the end.

Make a 4 cm cut along the middle of the right-hand half. Fold the lower piece down flat. Turn the paper over and turn the other half of the strip down.

Pick up the paper and straighten out the two wider pieces, to make a T-shape.

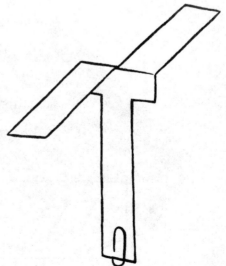

Hold the helicopter by the paperclipped leg above your head and let it go. Watch those blades whirl!

Top tip: Try adding more paper clips to make your helicopter spin and fall faster.

Fairground Fun

Roll up, roll up and enjoy your very own fairground attraction. See who has the best aim when taking a pot shot!

You will need:

• 4 empty six-packs of yogurts
(each of the pots must be big enough to fit a ping-pong ball and make sure the pots are still joined together)
• a large cardboard box measuring
at least 30 cm by 45 cm • five ping-pong balls
• coloured acrylic paints • scissors • glue • masking tape

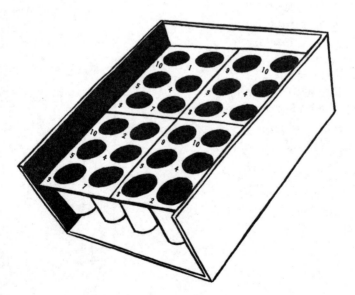

Tape the four yogurt six-packs into a rectangle (as shown in the picture opposite). These are your targets.

Paint the top of each six-pack a different colour. Devise your own scoring system by painting a number between one and ten next to each hole. Leave the pots to dry.

Meanwhile, cut off the front and top of the cardboard box. Glue the bottoms of the yogurt pots inside the cardboard box.

To make your target board tilt towards you, put a couple of books under the end of the box.

Stand at a specified distance from your target board (younger players can be a little closer than others) and take turns in seeing who can score the highest number of points by throwing five ping-pong balls.

Indoor And Outdoor Games

Long ago, when Dad was young, he couldn't always play outside because of the sabre-toothed tigers and woolly mammoths that roamed the Earth. Here are some games that are great to play when you are stuck indoors, and one to play when the coast is clear outside.

SARDINES

This game is hide-and-seek in reverse and it is usually played indoors.

One person hides, while everyone else counts to 50 very slowly. To stop people from rattling through the numbers too fast, you must count, 'One-tyrannosaurus, two-diplodocus, three-tyrannosaurus,' all the way to 50.

Then the seekers split up and start hunting. If a seeker finds the person that is hiding, they squash in next to them in the hiding place.

The loser is the last person to find the hiding place where all the other players are squashed together like sardines in a can.

DUCK DAD GOOSE

This is another great indoor game for four players or more. Dad is the 'goose' and the other players are 'ducks'. The ducks sit in a circle on the floor while Dad prowls around the circle.

When he touches one of the duck's shoulders, that duck has to leap to their feet. Both the duck and the goose sprint round the circle until they return to the empty space. The first person back to the empty space sits down. The person still standing becomes the goose.

FORTY-FORTY

This is an outdoor game. Choose a base, such as a lamp-post or a tree. One person is picked to be the hunter. Let's say Dad is chosen for the first round. The object of the game is to hide while Dad counts to 40. When Dad leaves the base to start looking, the hunted need to try to get back to base without being caught.

Dad doesn't have to touch the players to catch them out – he just has to see them, then run back to base and shout, 'Forty-forty, I see you!', and name them.

If the hunted can run fast and beat him back to base, they are safe. The last person to be caught is the next hunter.

ALSO AVAILABLE:

THINGS TO DO WITH MUM
ISBN: 978-1-906082-19-2